RISING ABOVE THE SHADOWS

Overcoming Self-Sabotage, Depression, and Anxiety

Kimberly Hodge

ISBN: 9798853521605

Cover design by: Canva
Printed in the United States of America

DISCLAIMER

Information provided in this book is for informative purposes only. Reader should discuss his or her physical, emotional, and mental issues with a medical professional or their primary care physician.

Reader agrees to hold harmless the author and publisher for any and all liability. Author has not verified all information provided within this book obtained through third parties.

Always consult with a medical professional before incorporating any new app or gadget into your mental health management plan.

INTRODUCTION

In the darkest moments of our lives, when self-sabotage, depression, and anxiety seem to hold us captive in a suffocating embrace, it is essential to remember that there is always a glimmer of hope waiting to be discovered.

Encouragement becomes our guiding light amidst the shadows, reminding us that we possess an inner strength capable of conquering even the fiercest battles within ourselves.

As we navigate this treacherous journey towards overcoming our demons, let inspiration serve as our faithful companion - an unwavering voice whispering words of resilience and determination into our weary souls.

It is during these times that we must realize the immense power lying dormant within us; the power to rise above adversity and rewrite our own stories. Though darkness may cloud our minds and heavy burdens rest upon our shoulders, know that this too shall pass.

Embrace each day as an opportunity for growth and healing – a chance to prove not only to others but also ourselves that we are capable of transcending all limitations set before us. With every step forward on this path towards liberation from self-sabotage, depression, and anxiety, let courage be your armor while hope fuels your spirit.

Remember: you are not alone in this struggle; countless others have walked similar paths and emerged victorious against their own internal battles.

So today, take heart in knowing that despite how insurmountable it may appear now – through encouragement's gentle touch - your story will inspire others who face similar struggles along their own voyage.

CONTENTS

CHAPTER 1: UNDERSTANDING SELF-SABOTAGE

Have you ever found yourself taking one step forward and two steps back? Or perhaps, despite your best intentions, you consistently find ways to undermine your own success?

If so, you may be caught in the web of Self-Sabotage. This destructive behavior can creep into every aspect of our lives - from personal relationships to professional endeavors.

But fear not! In this book, we will delve deep into the psychology behind Self-Sabotage, explore its causes and symptoms, and most importantly, uncover practical strategies to break free from its grip. So, buckle up as we embark on a journey of self-discovery and empowerment!

What is Self-Sabotage?

Self-Sabotage is like a hidden saboteur lurking within us, sabotaging our own goals and desires without us even realizing it. It's the internal battle between what we consciously want to achieve and the subconscious patterns of behavior that hold us back. It's that nagging voice in our heads whispering doubt and fear into our ears.

At its core, Self-Sabotage is a defense mechanism. It stems from deeply ingrained beliefs about us - beliefs that often stem from past experiences or negative programming. These beliefs convince us that we are unworthy of success or happiness, leading us to engage in behaviors that undermine our progress.

The tricky thing about Self-Sabotage is that it can manifest in many different ways. It could be procrastination - putting off tasks until the last minute, despite knowing they need to be done. Or it could be perfectionism - setting impossibly high standards for us and feeling crushed when we inevitably fall short.

Another common form of Self-Sabotage is chronic self-doubt. We second-guess every decision, constantly seeking validation from others instead of trusting our own judgment. And let's not forget about the classic "fear of failure" trap, where we avoid taking risks altogether to protect ourselves from potential disappointment.

No matter how Self-Sabotage shows up in your life, one thing remains clear: it holds you back from reaching your full potential and living a fulfilled life. But fear not! In the following sections, we will explore how to identify these destructive patterns and provide actionable strategies to overcome them once and for all!

Causes of Self Sabotaging Behavior

Understanding the causes of self-sabotaging behavior is crucial in breaking free from its grip. While everyone's experiences and triggers may differ, there are some common underlying factors that contribute to this destructive pattern.

One possible cause is rooted in fear and low self-esteem. When we doubt our abilities or feel unworthy of success, we may unconsciously sabotage ourselves to avoid facing potential failure or disappointment. This fear of rejection or judgment can hold us back from taking risks and pursuing our goals wholeheartedly.

Another factor could be past traumas or negative experiences that have shaped our beliefs about ourselves. These deeply ingrained patterns can manifest as Self-Sabotage, as we unknowingly repeat destructive behaviors or push away opportunities for growth and happiness.

Additionally, perfectionism plays a significant role in Self-Sabotage. The relentless pursuit of flawlessness often leads to feelings of inadequacy and an overwhelming fear of making mistakes. Consequently, we may engage in self-defeating behaviors rather than accepting imperfections and embracing progress over perfection.

Moreover, external influences such as societal expectations or toxic relationships can fuel Self-Sabotage tendencies. Trying to meet unrealistic standards set by others might lead to feelings of overwhelm and the belief that success is unattainable. Similarly, being surrounded by unsupportive individuals who discourage our ambitions can sabotage our efforts before they even begin.

It's important to note that these causes are not exhaustive but provide insights into the complex nature behind self-sabotaging behavior. By recognizing these underlying factors within us, we can start working towards breaking free from this cycle and creating a more fulfilling life filled with joy and success

Symptoms of Self-Sabotage

Self-Sabotage can manifest in various ways, and recognizing the symptoms is crucial for understanding and addressing this behavior. Here are some common signs that you may be engaging in self-sabotaging patterns:

1. **Procrastination:** Do you find yourself constantly putting off important tasks or delaying actions that could lead to your success? Procrastination is a classic symptom of Self-Sabotage, as it allows us to avoid facing our fears or taking responsibility.

2. **Perfectionism:** While striving for excellence is admirable, perfectionism can become detrimental when it prevents us from moving forward or taking risks. Constantly seeking flawless outcomes can lead to paralysis and missed opportunities.

3. **Negative self-talk:** If your inner dialogue is filled with self-doubt, criticism, and pessimistic thoughts, it's likely that you're undermining your own progress. Negative self-talk erodes confidence and reinforces limiting beliefs.

4. **Fear of failure (or success):** Fear often drives self-sabotaging behavior. Whether it's a fear of failing and being judged or a fear of succeeding and having to navigate unfamiliar territory, these fears can hold us back from reaching our full potential.

5. **Self-destructive habits:** Engaging in destructive behaviors such as excessive drinking, overeating, overspending, or unhealthy relationships can be indicative of deeper issues related to Self-Sabotage. These behaviors provide temporary relief but ultimately hinder personal growth.

6. **Self-Sabotage at work/home life balance:** Maintaining a healthy work-life balance is essential for overall well-being; however, Self-Sabotage may cause individuals working too much without breaks leading them into burnout while others neglect their responsibilities because they feel overwhelmed by

the demands placed upon them which leads them down an unproductive path diminishing their sense fulfillment.

By recognizing these symptoms within ourselves and reflecting on how they impact our lives, we can begin to break free from the cycle of Self-Sabotage. Stay tuned for the next section where we explore strategies to overcome self-sabotaging

The Psychological Impact of Self-Sabotage

The psychological impact of Self-Sabotage can be profound and far-reaching. When we engage in self-sabotaging behaviors, we undermine our own success and happiness, leading to feelings of frustration, disappointment, and a sense of being stuck.

One of the primary psychological impacts is a negative self-image. Self-Sabotage often stems from deep-rooted beliefs that we are unworthy or incapable of achieving our goals. This negative self-perception can affect every aspect of our lives, leading to low self-esteem, lack of confidence, and a constant fear of failure.

Self-Sabotage also takes a toll on our mental health. The cycle of setting goals and then sabotaging we creates a sense of internal conflict and confusion. We may experience increased levels of anxiety, stress, and even depression as we struggle with the consequences of our own actions.

Furthermore, Self-Sabotage can erode trust in ourselves. Each time we give in to destructive behaviors or make choices that go against our best interests, we lose faith in our ability to make wise decisions or create positive change in our lives.

In addition to these internal struggles, the psychological impact extends into our relationships as well. Self-sabotaging behavior can strain friendships and romantic partnerships as others may become frustrated by the inconsistency or unpredictability that comes with it.

Understanding the psychological impact is crucial for recognizing patterns within us and taking steps towards breaking free from this damaging cycle. It's important to remember that acknowledging and addressing these issues is the first step towards healing and personal growth

Examples of Self Sabotaging Behavior

Self-Sabotage can manifest in various ways, often without us even realizing it. Here are a few examples of common self-sabotaging behaviors that many people may experience:

1. **Procrastination:** Putting off tasks or responsibilities until the last minute, leading to increased stress and decreased productivity.

2. **Negative self-talk:** Constantly criticizing oneself, doubting abilities, and focusing on weaknesses rather than strengths.

3. **Fear of failure:** Avoiding new challenges or opportunities due to a fear of not succeeding or being judged by others.

4. **Perfectionism:** Setting impossibly high standards for oneself and becoming paralyzed by the fear of making mistakes.

5. **People-pleasing:** Prioritizing the needs and desires of others over one's own, which can lead to feelings of resentment and neglecting personal goals.

6. **Self-medication:** Using substances such as drugs or alcohol as a coping mechanism to escape negative emotions or situations temporarily.

7. **Impulsive behavior:** Acting on immediate gratification without considering long-term consequences, resulting in regret and missed opportunities.

8. **Sabotaging relationships:** Pushing away loved ones through trust issues, jealousy, or emotional manipulation due to underlying insecurities or fears of intimacy.

It is important to remember that everyone may exhibit different forms of Self-Sabotage based on their unique experiences and psychological makeup. Recognizing these patterns is the first step towards overcoming them and creating positive change in our lives!

How to Stop Self Sabotaging

It's time to break free from the cycle of Self-Sabotage and start living your best life. Here are some strategies that can help you overcome this destructive behavior.

First, it's important to identify the underlying reasons for your self-sabotaging tendencies. This could be rooted in fear, low self-esteem, or past traumas. Once you understand the root cause, you can begin working on addressing these issues head-on.

Next, practice self-awareness and mindfulness. Pay attention to your thoughts and actions, noticing when they veer towards self-destructive patterns. By being aware of these tendencies, you can interrupt them before they take hold.

Another effective strategy is setting realistic goals and breaking them down into manageable steps. This helps prevent overwhelm and allows for small victories along the way.

Additionally, surround yourself with a supportive network of friends or family who believe in your potential and will encourage positive change. Seek out mentors or therapists who can provide guidance and accountability on your journey towards overcoming Self-Sabotage.

Prioritize self-care activities that nourish both your mind and body. Engage in activities that bring joy and fulfillment while also promoting personal growth.

Remember, stopping self-sabotaging behaviors takes time and effort but with perseverance and dedication, you have the power to break free from this destructive cycle!

Seeking Professional Help for Self-Sabotage

When it comes to overcoming self-sabotaging behavior, sometimes seeking professional help can be the best course of action. While it's important to acknowledge that everyone's journey is different, working with a trained therapist or counselor can provide valuable insights and strategies to address Self-Sabotage patterns.

A skilled professional will create a safe and non-judgmental space for you to explore the underlying causes of your self-destructive behaviors. Through targeted questioning and active listening, they can help uncover deep-rooted beliefs and traumas that may be contributing to your Self-Sabotage.

Therapists often use various evidence-based techniques such as Cognitive Behavioral Therapy (CBT) or Dialectical Behavior Therapy (DBT) to challenge negative thought patterns and develop healthier coping mechanisms. They will guide you in setting realistic goals, breaking down overwhelming tasks into manageable steps, and holding yourself accountable.

Additionally, therapy provides an opportunity for personal growth and increased self-awareness. By understanding the triggers that lead to Self-Sabotage, you can learn new ways of responding to challenging situations effectively.

Remember, seeking professional help is not a sign of weakness but rather a courageous step towards healing and personal transformation. If you feel like your self-sabotaging behaviors are negatively impacting your life or relationships, reaching out for support from a qualified mental health professional can make all the difference on your path towards positive change.

Resources for Understanding and Coping with Self-Sabotage

If you've recognized that self-sabotaging behavior is holding you bac K, here are some helpful resources to explore from reaching your full potential, it's important to seek the necessary resources to understand and overcome this pattern. Here are some valuable resources that can help:

1. **Books:** There are several books available on Self-Sabotage that offer insights into its causes and provide practical strategies for breaking free from this detrimental cycle. Some recommended titles include "The Big Leap" by Gay Hendricks, "Breaking the Habit of Being Yourself" by Dr. Joe Dispenza, and "Self-Sabotage Syndrome" by Janet Geringer Woititz.

2. **Therapy or Counseling:** Seeking professional help from a therapist or counselor who specializes in personal growth and behavioral patterns can be immensely beneficial in addressing self-sabotaging tendencies. They can guide you through the process of identifying underlying issues, developing coping mechanisms, and creating an action plan for positive change.

3. **Support Groups:** Joining a support group or attending workshops focused on Self-Sabotage can provide a sense of community where individuals share similar experiences and challenges. This avenue allows for open discussions, learning from others' journeys, gaining new perspectives, and receiving encouragement along the way.

4. **Mindfulness Practices:** Incorporating mindfulness practices such as meditation or journaling into your daily routine can cultivate greater awareness of your thoughts, emotions, and behaviors related to Self-Sabotage. These practices enhance your ability to recognize triggers before they lead to harmful actions while promoting self-reflection and inner growth.

5. **Online Resources:** The internet offers numerous online forums, articles, podcasts, videos, and courses dedicated to understanding self-sabotaging behavior better and providing guidance on overcoming it effectively.

Remember that overcoming Self-Sabotage is not an overnight process - it requires commitment, patience with yourself during setbacks, and consistent effort towards positive change. By utilizing these resources and implementing the strategies they offer, you can

How to Overcome Self-Sabotage

Overcoming Self-Sabotage can be a challenging journey, but it is not impossible. Here are some strategies that can help you break free from this destructive pattern.

1. **Increase Self-Awareness:** The first step in overcoming Self-Sabotage is to become aware of your behaviors and thought patterns. Pay attention to the moments when you engage in self-defeating actions or negative self-talk.

2. **Challenge Negative Beliefs:** Often, self-sabotaging behavior stems from deep-rooted negative beliefs about us or our abilities. Challenge these beliefs by questioning their validity and replacing them with more positive and empowering thoughts.

3. **Set Realistic Goals:** Setting unrealistic goals can set you up for failure and trigger self-sabotaging behavior. Instead, set small, achievable goals that will boost your confidence gradually.

4. **Practice Self-Compassion:** It's important to treat yourself with kindness and understanding throughout this process. Be gentle with yourself when setbacks occur, as they are a natural part of growth.

5. **Create Supportive Relationships:** Surround yourself with people who believe in your potential and provide encouragement on your journey towards success.

6. **Seek Professional Help if Needed:** If Self-Sabotage continues to hinder your progress despite your best efforts, don't hesitate to seek support from a therapist or counselor who specializes in personal development.

Remember that overcoming Self-Sabotage takes time and effort; be patient with yourself as you work towards creating positive change in your life.

The Impact of Self-Sabotage on Success

Are you your own worst enemy when it comes to achieving success? Do you find yourself constantly getting in your own way, sabotaging your efforts and holding yourself back from reaching your goals? If so, you're not alone. Self-Sabotage is a common phenomenon that affects countless individuals across the globe.

In this book, we'll delve into the definition of Self-Sabotage, explore its psychological underpinnings, discuss common forms of self-sabotaging behavior, and most importantly, examine its profound impact on success. So, buckle up and get ready to uncover the secrets behind Self-Sabotage and learn how to break free from its clutches once and for all!

The Definition of Self-Sabotage

Self-Sabotage, in its simplest form, refers to the act of consciously or unconsciously sabotaging one's own progress and success. It is like shooting oneself in the foot just as you're about to cross the finish line. This self-destructive behavior often stems from deep-rooted fears, insecurities, and negative beliefs that we hold about ourselves.

At its core, Self-Sabotage is a defense mechanism that arises from a fear of failure or rejection. We may subconsciously believe that if we try our best and still fall short, it confirms our deepest fears - that we are not good enough or worthy of success.

By engaging in self-sabotaging behaviors such as procrastination, self-doubt, perfectionism, or even pushing people away when they get too close to us emotionally or professionally, we inadvertently create obstacles on our path to achievement.

It's important to recognize that Self-Sabotage can manifest differently for each individual. For some people, it may manifest as imposter syndrome - constantly feeling like a fraud despite evidence of their accomplishments. Others may engage in negative thought patterns where they consistently undermine their abilities and downplay their achievements.

Regardless of how it presents itself in your life, the impact of Self-Sabotage on success cannot be underestimated. It acts as an invisible force holding you back from reaching your full potential and achieving your goals. It becomes a vicious cycle where every step forward is followed by two steps backward.

The consequences of Self-Sabotage extend beyond thwarting personal goals; it can also affect relationships and professional opportunities. Constantly doubting yourself can lead others to doubt you as well, hindering collaboration and limiting advancement possibilities.

Now that we understand what Self-Sabotage entails let's explore how this destructive pattern can be overcome so that you can break free from its grip on your life once and for all!

The Psychology Behind Self-Sabotage

The psychology behind Self-Sabotage is complex and can vary from person to person. It often stems from deep-rooted beliefs, fears, and insecurities that we may not even be aware of. At its core, Self-Sabotage involves engaging in behaviors or thought patterns that undermine our own success or well-being.

One common psychological factor behind Self-Sabotage is a fear of failure. We may unconsciously sabotage ourselves because we are afraid of what might happen if we actually succeed. This fear can stem from a lack of confidence or a belief that we don't deserve success.

Another psychological aspect at play is the need for control. By sabotaging ourselves, we maintain a sense of control over our lives, even if it means sacrificing our goals or dreams. This need for control may come from past experiences where we felt powerless or out of control.

Self-Sabotage can also be influenced by negative self-beliefs and low self-esteem. If we have internalized negative messages about ourselves, such as "I'm not good enough" or "I always mess things up," then these beliefs can drive us to engage in behaviors that reinforce those beliefs.

Furthermore, unresolved emotional issues and traumas can contribute to self-sabotaging behavior. These unresolved issues create underlying emotional pain that drives us to sabotage ourselves as a way to cope with or avoid facing those painful emotions.

Understanding the psychology behind Self-Sabotage is an important step towards overcoming it and achieving success in various aspects of life. By identifying the underlying factors driving our sabotaging behaviors, we can begin to challenge and change them.

Note: The word count for this blog section is 193 words before removing repetitive phrases

Common Forms of Self-Sabotaging Behavior

Self-Sabotage can manifest in various ways, often without us even realizing it. Understanding these common forms of self-sabotaging behavior is crucial for recognizing and addressing them.

One common form of Self-Sabotage is procrastination. We delay taking action on important tasks or goals, which ultimately hinders our progress and success. Another form is negative self-talk, where we constantly criticize ourselves and doubt our abilities.

Perfectionism also falls into the category of Self-Sabotage. When we strive for perfection, we set unrealistic standards that are impossible to meet, leading to frustration and a fear of failure.

Another destructive behavior is excessive people-pleasing. Constantly seeking validation from others can prevent us from prioritizing our own needs and pursuing our ambitions.

Imposter syndrome is another prevalent form of Self-Sabotage. Despite evidence of competence or accomplishments, individuals with imposter syndrome believe they are frauds who will be exposed as failures at any moment.

Engaging in harmful coping mechanisms like overeating, substance abuse or excessive spending can also be forms of Self-Sabotage used to numb emotions temporarily but hinder long-term growth.

Understanding these common behaviors allows us to identify when we may be sabotaging ourselves and take steps towards healthier habits and increased success. By recognizing these patterns early on, we can work towards overcoming them and achieving the personal and professional fulfillment we desire.

The Impact of Self-Sabotage on Success

Self-Sabotage can have a profound impact on our ability to achieve success. It is a self-destructive behavior that hinders our progress and holds us back from reaching our full potential. This detrimental habit can manifest in various ways, such as procrastination, negative self-talk, fear of failure, and perfectionism.

When we engage in self-sabotaging behaviors, we undermine our own efforts and sabotage the opportunities that come our way. We may start projects with enthusiasm only to abandon them halfway through or consistently doubt ourselves and question whether we deserve success. These actions create a cycle of frustration and disappointment that prevents us from realizing our goals.

The consequences of Self-Sabotage are far-reaching. It not only affects our professional life but also seeps into other areas like relationships, health, and overall well-being. Constantly sabotaging we erodes confidence and creates a negative mindset that becomes difficult to break free from.

To overcome this destructive pattern, it is important to identify the root causes behind your self-sabotaging behaviors. Reflecting on past experiences or seeking support from professionals can help you gain insights into why you engage in these damaging habits.

Developing strategies to counteract Self-Sabotage is crucial for achieving success. Setting realistic goals, practicing positive affirmations, breaking tasks into smaller steps, and surrounding yourself with supportive individuals are effective ways to combat this tendency.

Remember that overcoming Self-Sabotage takes time and effort. Be patient with yourself as you work towards breaking free from these patterns of behavior.

By conquering Self-Sabotage tendencies head-on, you will open doors for personal growth and create opportunities for true success in all aspects of your life.

Overcoming Self-Sabotage at Work

Self-Sabotage can be especially detrimental in the workplace, where it can hinder career growth and success. Fortunately, there are strategies you can employ to overcome self-sabotaging behavior and thrive in your professional life.

It's important to identify the underlying causes of your Self-Sabotage. Are you afraid of failure or success? Do you have limiting beliefs about your abilities? By addressing these root causes, you can begin to challenge and change them.

Setting realistic goals is another crucial step in overcoming Self-Sabotage at work. Break down larger tasks into manageable steps and celebrate each small accomplishment along the way. This will boost your confidence and keep you motivated.

Building a support network is also essential for overcoming Self-Sabotage. Surround yourself with positive and supportive colleagues who believe in your abilities. Seek out mentors or coaches who can provide guidance and encouragement as you navigate challenges.

Additionally, practicing mindfulness can help counteract self-sabotaging thoughts and behaviors. Take time each day to check in with yourself, reflect on any negative patterns that may arise, and consciously choose more empowering thoughts instead.

Don't be afraid to seek professional help if needed. A therapist or counselor trained in cognitive-behavioral therapy (CBT) techniques can assist you in developing healthier thought patterns and coping strategies specific to your work environment.

By taking proactive steps towards overcoming Self-Sabotage at work, you'll position yourself for greater success, satisfaction, and fulfillment in your career journey

Overcoming Self-Sabotage in Relationships

Building and maintaining healthy relationships can be challenging, especially when self-sabotaging behaviors come into play. If you find yourself constantly pushing away potential partners or sabotaging existing relationships, it's essential to take a step back and reflect on your actions. Here are some strategies to help you overcome Self-Sabotage in relationships.

Gaining awareness of your patterns is crucial. Take the time to identify any recurring negative thoughts or behaviors that tend to sabotage your relationships. By understanding these patterns, you can begin to challenge them and replace them with healthier alternatives.

Next, practice self-compassion and acceptance. It's important not to beat yourself up over past mistakes or perceived flaws. Instead, focus on accepting yourself for who you are and embracing personal growth.

Communication plays a vital role in overcoming Self-Sabotage in relationships. Openly express your feelings, needs, and concerns with your partner while also being willing to listen actively. Effective communication fosters trust and strengthens the bond between partners.

Additionally, setting boundaries is essential for maintaining healthy dynamics within a relationship. Clearly define what is acceptable behavior for both parties involved and communicate those boundaries respectfully.

Working on building self-esteem is another key aspect of overcoming Self-Sabotage in relationships. Develop confidence in yourself by engaging in activities that make you happy and fulfill your personal goals outside of the relationship.

Seek support from trusted friends or consider therapy if needed. A professional therapist can provide valuable guidance as they help you navigate through any underlying issues contributing to self-sabotaging behavior.

By implementing these strategies consistently and remaining committed to personal growth, it becomes possible to break free from destructive patterns of Self-Sabotage within romantic relationships.

CHAPTER 2: DECODING DEPRESSION

Feeling down, unmotivated, or just not like yourself lately? You're not alone. Depression is a common yet often misunderstood condition that affects millions of people worldwide. Whether you've experienced it firsthand or know someone who has, understanding depression is key to finding support and navigating the road to recovery.

In this book, we'll dive deep into the world of depression – decoding its symptoms, exploring its causes and contributing factors, discussing diagnosis and treatment options, sharing self-care strategies for coping, and shedding light on related conditions. Plus, we'll provide valuable resources and support networks to help you or your loved ones on their journey towards healing.

So grab a cup of tea (or coffee!) and join me as we unravel the complexities of depression. Together, let's empower ourselves with knowledge and discover hope in even the darkest moments. The path ahead may be challenging at times but remember there is always light at the end of the tunnel!

Overview

Depression is more than just feeling sad or having a down day. It is a complex mental health condition that can affect every aspect of a person's life. From their thoughts and emotions to their physical well-being, depression casts a long shadow over daily existence.

At its core, depression is characterized by persistent feelings of sadness, hopelessness, and a loss of interest in once-enjoyable activities. These symptoms can be overwhelming and make even the simplest tasks feel like monumental challenges.

Depression doesn't discriminate – it can affect anyone regardless of age, gender, or background. While some people may experience only one episode of depression in their lifetime, others may battle with recurrent bouts that disrupt their lives for years.

It's important to understand that depression is not simply a matter of "snapping out" of it or having a positive attitude. It's an illness that requires compassion, understanding, and appropriate treatment. With the right support system in place and access to professional help, individuals living with depression can find relief and regain control over their lives.

In the next sections of this blog post, we will explore the various symptoms associated with depression depending on age groups such as children/teens and older adults. We will also discuss when it might be necessary to seek medical attention or emergency help if you or someone you know is experiencing severe depressive symptoms.

Stay tuned as we delve into the causes and contributing factors behind this pervasive condition so we can better comprehend why it affects us differently. Remember: knowledge is power when it comes to tackling our mental health struggles head-on!

Symptoms

Symptoms of depression can vary from person to person, but there are some common signs to watch out for. These symptoms may manifest differently in children and teens compared to older adults.

In children and teens, symptoms of depression often include persistent sadness or irritability, withdrawal from friends and activities they used to enjoy, changes in appetite or sleep patterns, difficulty concentrating or making decisions, feelings of worthlessness or guilt, and even thoughts of death or suicide.

For older adults, symptoms may be more subtle. They might experience a loss of interest in hobbies or socializing, changes in appetite or weight loss/gain, trouble sleeping or excessive sleeping, fatigue or lack of energy, feelings of hopelessness or pessimism , slowed thinking/mental processes , unexplained physical ailments like headaches or stomachaches ,and thoughts of self-harm.

It's important to note that experiencing one symptom does not necessarily mean someone has depression. A diagnosis should be made by a healthcare professional based on the presence and duration of multiple symptoms.

If you suspect that you or someone you know is experiencing these symptoms consistently over a period of time - it's important to reach out for help!

Symptoms in Children and Teens

Symptoms in children and teens can often be different from those experienced by adults. It is crucial for parents, teachers, and caregivers to recognize these signs early on to provide the necessary support.

In younger children, depression may manifest as irritability or frequent tantrums. They may also exhibit changes in appetite or sleep patterns. Additionally, they might complain of physical symptoms like stomachaches or headaches without any underlying medical cause.

Teens, on the other hand, may display more classic symptoms such as persistent sadness or feelings of hopelessness. They may lose interest in activities they once enjoyed and withdraw from friends or family members. Poor academic performance and a decline in personal hygiene are also common indicators.

It's important to note that not all young people will experience every symptom mentioned above. Each individual's experience with depression can vary greatly.

If you suspect your child or teen may be struggling with depression, it is vital to seek professional help promptly. A qualified healthcare provider can evaluate their symptoms and recommend appropriate treatment options tailored to their specific needs. Remember that timely intervention can make a significant difference in their well-being and overall quality of life.

Symptoms in Older Adults

Symptoms in older adults can manifest differently than in other age groups, making it important to recognize the unique signs of depression in this population. While some symptoms may overlap with those experienced by younger individuals, there are specific indicators that are more prevalent among older adults.

One common symptom is persistent sadness or a feeling of emptiness. Older adults may also experience a loss of interest or pleasure in activities they once enjoyed. Sleep disturbances, such as insomnia or excessive sleeping, can be another sign of depression.

Physical symptoms like fatigue and changes in appetite are frequently reported by older adults with depression. They may also complain of unexplained physical pain or digestive issues.

Cognitive symptoms can include difficulty concentrating, memory problems, and slowed thinking processes. Older adults might exhibit irritability or express feelings of worthlessness or guilt as well.

It's essential to note that these symptoms can vary from person to person, and not all older adults will display every symptom. If you notice any significant changes in mood or behavior that persist for an extended period, it's crucial to encourage your loved one to seek professional help for proper diagnosis and treatment options available for them.

When to See a Doctor

When to see a doctor for depression? It's an important question that shouldn't be taken lightly. While everyone experiences sadness and low moods at times, it's crucial to recognize when these feelings become persistent and interfere with daily life.

If you or someone you know is experiencing any of the following symptoms, it may be time to seek professional help:

1. **Prolonged sadness or emptiness:** Feeling down for an extended period, with little relief even after engaging in activities that used to bring joy.

2. **Changes in appetite and weight:** Significant changes in eating habits, such as overeating or loss of appetite leading to noticeable weight gain or loss.

3. **Sleep disturbances:** Difficulty falling asleep, staying asleep, or excessive sleeping patterns that disrupt normal sleep routines.

4. **Loss of interest:** Losing interest in previously enjoyed activities like hobbies, socializing, or personal relationships.

5. **Fatigue and lack of energy:** Persistent feelings of exhaustion and decreased motivation despite getting enough rest.

6. **Physical symptoms without medical cause:** Experiencing unexplained physical pains like headaches or stomachaches without any underlying medical condition.

7. **Feelings of worthlessness or guilt:** Constant self-criticism and negative thoughts about oneself accompanied by overwhelming guilt.

8. **Difficulty concentrating and making decisions:** Trouble focusing on tasks at hand and experiencing challenges when making even simple choices.

It's essential not to delay seeking professional help if you notice these signs persisting for more than two weeks. A mental health specialist can provide an accurate diagnosis and develop a personalized treatment plan tailored to your needs.

When to Get Emergency Help

When it comes to mental health, knowing when to seek help is crucial. In the case of depression, there are certain situations that require immediate attention and emergency assistance.

If you or someone you know is experiencing any of the following symptoms, it's important to call for help right away:

1. **Suicidal thoughts or plans:** If thoughts of self-harm or suicide are present, reach out for immediate support. There are helplines available 24/7 where trained professionals can provide guidance and resources.

2. **Intense feelings of hopelessness or despair:** Feeling overwhelmed by negative emotions can be a sign that professional intervention is needed urgently.

3. **Sudden changes in behavior:** Rapid shifts in mood, increased agitation or aggression may indicate a crisis situation requiring immediate attention.

4. **Loss of touch with reality:** Experiencing hallucinations or delusions could signify an acute psychiatric episode that needs urgent evaluation and treatment.

Remember, seeking emergency help doesn't mean you're weak or incapable; it means prioritizing your well-being and safety above all else. Don't hesitate to reach out if you believe someone's life is at risk due to depression-related symptoms.

Causes and Contributing Factors

Depression is a complex condition that can be influenced by various causes and contributing factors. While it's important to note that everyone's experience with depression is unique, there are some common elements that can play a role in its development.

Biological factors may contribute to the onset of depression. Imbalances in brain chemicals, such as serotonin and dopamine, have been linked to depressive symptoms. Additionally, genetic predisposition can make certain individuals more susceptible to developing depression.

Environmental factors also play a significant role in triggering or exacerbating depressive episodes. Traumatic life events, such as loss of a loved one, relationship difficulties, or financial stressors, can act as triggers for depression. Chronic exposure to stressful situations or living in an unsupportive environment can also contribute to the development of this mental health condition.

Psychological factors cannot be overlooked when discussing the causes of depression. Individuals who have low self-esteem or struggle with negative thinking patterns may be more prone to experiencing depressive symptoms. Additionally, individuals with certain personality traits like perfectionism or high levels of anxiety may have an increased risk.

It's essential to recognize that these causes and contributing factors often interact with each other rather than acting alone. Understanding these complexities helps healthcare professionals tailor treatment plans specific to each individual's needs.

If you suspect you or someone you know may be struggling with depression, seeking professional help is crucial for accurate diagnosis and effective treatment strategies.

Diagnosis and Treatment

When it comes to depression, timely diagnosis and appropriate treatment are crucial. However, identifying depression can be challenging since its symptoms may vary from person to person. A healthcare professional will typically conduct a thorough evaluation to determine the presence of depressive episodes.

In terms of treatment, there are various options available depending on the severity and individual needs. Medication is often prescribed for moderate to severe cases of depression. Antidepressants work by restoring chemical imbalances in the brain that contribute to depressive symptoms.

Psychotherapy, or talk therapy, is another common approach used in treating depression. This therapeutic intervention aims at helping individuals understand their emotions better and develop coping strategies for managing them effectively.

In addition to medication and psychotherapy, there are other treatment options that can complement traditional approaches. These include lifestyle modifications such as regular exercise, healthy eating habits, stress reduction techniques like meditation or yoga, and support groups where individuals can connect with others who share similar experiences.

It's important to remember that seeking help is not a sign of weakness but rather a courageous step towards healing. If you suspect you or someone you know may be experiencing depression symptoms, don't hesitate to reach out for professional assistance.

Medication

Medication can be an important part of the treatment plan for depression. It is often prescribed to help manage symptoms and improve overall well-being. There are several types of medications available, each with its own benefits and potential side effects.

One common type of medication used to treat depression is antidepressants. These medications work by balancing chemicals in the brain that affect mood. They can take a few weeks to start working effectively, so it's important to be patient and give them time.

Another type of medication sometimes prescribed for depression is anti-anxiety medications or benzodiazepines. These drugs help reduce feelings of anxiety and can provide temporary relief from symptoms.

In some cases, a healthcare provider may recommend mood stabilizers or antipsychotic medications as part of the treatment plan. These medications are typically used when there are other underlying mental health conditions present alongside depression.

It's essential to remember that medication alone may not be enough to fully address depression. It is often most effective when combined with psychotherapy or counseling sessions.

Always consult with a healthcare professional before starting any new medication, as they will evaluate your specific needs and determine the best course of action for you.

Psychotherapy

Psychotherapy, also known as talk therapy or counseling, is a commonly used treatment for depression. It involves working with a trained therapist who provides support and guidance in order to help individuals manage their symptoms and improve their overall well-being.

During psychotherapy sessions, the therapist creates a safe and non-judgmental space where individuals can explore their thoughts, feelings, and behaviors related to depression. They may use various techniques such as cognitive-behavioral therapy (CBT), interpersonal therapy (IPT), or psychodynamic therapy.

CBT focuses on identifying negative thought patterns and replacing them with more positive and realistic ones. IPT aims at improving relationships and communication skills to reduce depressive symptoms. Psychodynamic therapy delves into unconscious patterns that may contribute to depression.

The duration of psychotherapy can vary depending on individual needs but typically ranges from several weeks to several months or longer. Regular sessions allow for ongoing progress evaluation as well as the opportunity to address any challenges that arise during the therapeutic process.

It's important to note that psychotherapy is not a one-size-fits-all approach; different approaches work better for different people. Therefore, finding the right therapist who specializes in treating depression is essential for optimal results.

With dedication and commitment from both the therapist and individual seeking treatment, psychotherapy can be an effective tool in managing depression by providing coping strategies, promoting self-awareness, fostering resilience, improving problem-solving skills, enhancing relationships, boosting self-esteem, and ultimately leading towards lasting recovery.

Other Treatment Options

In addition to medication and psychotherapy, there are several other treatment options available for individuals dealing with depression. These alternative approaches can be used alongside or in place of traditional treatments, depending on the individual's preferences and needs.

One such option is exercise. Physical activity has been shown to have a positive impact on mood by releasing endorphins, which are natural feel-good chemicals in the brain. Incorporating regular exercise into your routine can help reduce symptoms of depression and improve overall well-being.

Another alternative treatment is acupuncture. This ancient Chinese practice involves inserting thin needles into specific points on the body to promote balance and healing. While more research is needed, some studies suggest that acupuncture may be effective in reducing depressive symptoms.

Mindfulness meditation is another non-pharmacological approach that has gained popularity in recent years. By focusing attention on the present moment without judgment, individuals can learn to better manage their emotions and reduce stress levels.

Additionally, certain dietary changes may also have a positive impact on mental health. Consuming a balanced diet rich in fruits, vegetables, whole grains, lean proteins, and healthy fats provides essential nutrients that support brain function.

It's important to note that while these alternative treatments may offer benefits for some individuals with depression, they should not replace professional medical advice or prescribed treatments. It's always best to consult with a healthcare provider before starting any new form of treatment.

Remember that everyone's journey with depression is unique—what works for one person may not work for another. Finding the right combination of treatments often requires patience and open communication with healthcare professionals who can guide you towards an individualized plan tailored specifically to your needs.

Self-care and Coping Strategies

Taking care of yourself is crucial when you're dealing with depression. It may feel overwhelming at times but remember that even small steps can make a big difference in your well-being.

First and foremost, prioritize self-care activities that bring you joy and relaxation. Whether it's spending time outdoors, engaging in hobbies or creative outlets, or simply taking a warm bath – do things that nourish your soul.

Physical exercise is also a powerful tool for managing depression. Aim for regular movement – it could be as simple as going for a walk or practicing yoga. Exercise releases endorphins, the "feel-good" hormones, which can help boost your mood.

Establishing healthy routines can provide structure and stability during difficult times. Set realistic goals for each day and celebrate even the smallest achievements. Remember to take breaks when needed and practice mindfulness or deep breathing exercises to stay grounded.

Nurturing social connections is another essential aspect of self-care. Reach out to trusted friends or family members who can offer support and understanding. If face-to-face interactions are challenging, consider connecting through phone calls or online platforms.

Managing stress levels plays an important role in coping with depression. Find stress reduction techniques that work best for you – such as meditation, journaling, listening to music, or practicing relaxation exercises like progressive muscle relaxation.

Don't hesitate to seek professional help if you need it. Therapists and counselors can provide valuable guidance on coping strategies tailored specifically to your needs.

Remember: Self-care isn't selfish; it's necessary for your overall well-being!

Prevention and Risk Factors

When it comes to depression, prevention plays a crucial role in managing the condition. While it may not always be possible to prevent depression entirely, there are steps you can take to reduce your risk and promote better mental health.

One important factor in preventing depression is maintaining a healthy lifestyle. This includes eating a balanced diet, engaging in regular exercise, and getting enough sleep. These lifestyle choices can have a significant impact on your mood and overall well-being.

Another key aspect of prevention is managing stress effectively. Chronic stress can increase the likelihood of developing depression, so finding healthy ways to cope with stress is essential. This might include practicing relaxation techniques such as deep breathing or mindfulness meditation.

Building strong social connections is also vital for reducing the risk of depression. Maintaining meaningful relationships with family and friends provides emotional support and helps combat feelings of loneliness or isolation.

Additionally, recognizing and addressing potential risk factors can help mitigate the chances of developing depression. Some common risk factors include a family history of mental illness, experiencing trauma or abuse, substance abuse issues, chronic medical conditions, or certain medications.

By identifying these risk factors early on and seeking appropriate support or treatment when necessary, individuals can take proactive steps towards mitigating their vulnerability to depression.

Remember that everyone's journey with mental health is unique; what works for one person may not work for another.

It's crucial to consult with healthcare professionals who specialize in mental health if you have concerns about your own well-being or that of someone you care about.

Taking preventive measures against depression should be seen as an ongoing process rather than a one-time solution —a continuous commitment to self-care that ultimately contributes to better overall mental health outcomes.

Related Conditions

Depression is a complex mental health condition that can often be intertwined with other disorders and conditions. It's important to understand these related conditions in order to provide comprehensive support and treatment for individuals experiencing depression.

One common related condition is anxiety. Many people with depression also experience symptoms of anxiety, such as excessive worry, restlessness, and difficulty concentrating. Anxiety can exacerbate feelings of sadness and hopelessness, making it even more challenging to cope with depression.

Another related condition is substance abuse or addiction. Some individuals may turn to drugs or alcohol as a way to self-medicate their depressive symptoms. However, this only serves as a temporary escape and can worsen the overall mental health picture.

There are also physical health conditions that can coexist with depression. Chronic pain conditions like fibromyalgia or arthritis can contribute to feelings of fatigue and low mood. In turn, depression can make it difficult for individuals to manage their physical symptoms effectively.

Additionally, eating disorders such as anorexia nervosa or bulimia may occur alongside depression. These disorders involve distorted body image perceptions and unhealthy relationships with food, further complicating the individual's emotional well-being.

sleep disorders are frequently associated with depressive episodes. Insomnia or hypersomnia (excessive sleeping) can disrupt regular sleep patterns, leading to increased fatigue and worsening of depressive symptoms.

Understanding these related conditions allows healthcare

professionals to develop personalized treatment plans that address all aspects of an individual's mental and physical well-being. By taking a holistic approach to treatment, we have the best chance at helping those living with depression find relief and regain control over their lives.

Research and Statistics

Research and statistics play a crucial role in understanding the prevalence and impact of depression. By delving into these findings, we can gain valuable insights that help shape treatment approaches and improve overall mental health awareness.

Numerous studies have been conducted to examine the prevalence of depression worldwide. According to the World Health Organization (WHO), more than 264 million people suffer from depression globally. This staggering number highlights the urgent need for effective interventions and support systems.

Research has also revealed interesting patterns when it comes to gender differences in depression. Women are twice as likely as men to experience depressive symptoms, although this may be attributed to various factors including hormonal imbalances, societal pressures, and biological predispositions.

Furthermore, research has explored potential risk factors for developing depression. Traumatic life events such as loss or abuse, genetic predisposition, chronic illness, substance abuse, and social isolation have all been identified as contributing factors.

In recent years, there has been an increasing focus on studying the link between physical health conditions and depression. Research suggests that individuals with chronic illnesses such as diabetes or cardiovascular disease are at a higher risk of experiencing depressive symptoms.

Statistics also shed light on how untreated or under-treated depression can impact society at large. Depression is not only associated with increased healthcare costs but also affects productivity in workplaces due to absenteeism and decreased performance.

Ongoing research aims to uncover more effective treatments for different types of depressions while exploring innovative therapeutic approaches like transcranial magnetic stimulation (TMS) or ketamine infusion therapy. The goal is always to find personalized solutions that address each individual's unique needs.

By staying informed about ongoing research efforts surrounding depression treatment and prevention strategies, we can foster hope for better outcomes in mental health management moving forward. It is essential that we continue supporting scientific investigations aimed at deepening our understanding of this complex condition.

Resources and Support

Resources and support play a crucial role in helping individuals navigate through the challenges of depression. When it comes to finding assistance, there are various options available that can provide guidance, understanding, and a sense of community.

Support hotlines are a valuable resource for those seeking immediate help or someone to talk to. These helplines offer confidential support from trained professionals who can provide guidance and reassurance during difficult times.

Online support networks have also emerged as a popular avenue for individuals looking for a safe space to share their experiences with others who understand what they're going through. These forums allow people to connect with peers, exchange coping strategies, and gain insights into different treatment approaches.

For those who prefer digital solutions, there are recommended apps, products, and gadgets specifically designed to assist individuals in managing their depression symptoms. From meditation apps to mood tracking devices, these tools can be helpful additions to one's self-care routine.

Organizations dedicated to depression support exist worldwide and offer resources such as educational materials, workshops, and access to mental health professionals. Connecting with these organizations can provide individuals with additional knowledge about their condition while fostering connections within the community.

Retreats focused on mental well-being have gained popularity in recent years. These retreats offer participants an opportunity for introspection and healing in serene environments facilitated by experts specializing in various therapeutic modalities.

It is important to remember that everyone's journey is unique when it comes to managing depression. What works for one person may not work for another; therefore, exploring multiple avenues of support is essential. It is always advisable that individuals consult with healthcare professionals before making any decisions regarding treatment options or accessing specific resources.

Support Hotlines

Support hotlines can be a lifeline for individuals struggling with depression. These helplines provide immediate emotional support and guidance to those in need, offering a safe space to talk about their feelings and concerns. Whether you're feeling overwhelmed, lonely, or just need someone to listen, support hotlines are there 24/7 to lend an empathetic ear.

When you call a support hotline, you'll be connected with trained professionals who understand the complexities of depression. They can offer compassionate advice, coping strategies, and even referrals to local resources that can further assist you on your journey towards healing.

One of the great things about support hotlines is that they provide anonymity. You don't have to worry about judgment or stigma when reaching out for help. You can freely express yourself without fear of repercussions.

If talking on the phone feels daunting, many helplines also offer text-based services or online chat options. This way, you have flexibility in how you communicate and receive support.

Remember that seeking help is not a sign of weakness; it's an act of strength and self-care. Sometimes all it takes is one conversation with someone who understands to make a significant difference in your mental well-being.

Don't hesitate to reach out if you're feeling down or overwhelmed – there are people ready and willing to listen and help guide you through this challenging time.

Online Support Networks

Online support networks can be a lifeline for individuals struggling with depression. These virtual communities provide a safe space where people can connect, share their experiences, and offer support to one another. One of the advantages of online support networks is that they are available 24/7, allowing individuals to seek help and guidance at any time.

These platforms offer anonymity, which can be particularly helpful for those who may feel uncomfortable sharing their struggles in person. Connecting with others who have gone through similar experiences can provide validation and a sense of belonging. It's important to note that online support networks should not replace professional help but rather complement it.

There are various types of online support networks available, including forums, chat rooms, social media groups, and dedicated websites or apps specifically designed for mental health support. Each platform has its own unique features and community guidelines.

It's crucial to find an online support network that aligns with your specific needs and values. Take the time to research different platforms and read reviews from other users before joining. Remember that everyone's experience is different, so finding the right fit may require some trial-and-error.

When participating in an online support network, it's essential to maintain healthy boundaries and prioritize self-care. While these communities can be incredibly supportive, it's important not to rely solely on them for all your emotional needs.

In conclusion (not conclusive), online support networks can be a valuable resource for individuals dealing with depression by providing connection, understanding, and encouragement from like-minded individuals facing similar challenges

Recommended apps, products, and gadgets

In today's digital age, there are numerous apps, products, and gadgets that aim to assist individuals dealing with depression. These tools can provide additional support and resources right at your fingertips. Here are a few recommendations:

1. **Mood tracking apps:** Many mobile applications allow you to track your mood on a daily basis. They provide a platform for you to record your emotions and identify patterns over time.

2. **Meditation apps:** Mindfulness meditation has been shown to have positive effects on mental health. There are various meditation apps available that offer guided sessions tailored specifically for managing depression symptoms.

3. **Light therapy devices:** Light therapy is often used as a treatment for seasonal affective disorder (SAD), but it can also be beneficial for individuals with depression. Light therapy devices mimic natural sunlight and may help regulate the body's internal clock.

4. **Wearable tech:** Several wearable devices now include features designed to monitor physical activity levels, sleep quality, heart rate variability, and stress levels - all of which can impact mental well-being.

It's important to note that while these tools can be helpful additions to your self-care routine, they should not replace professional treatment or advice from healthcare providers. Always consult with a medical professional before incorporating any new app or gadget into your depression management plan.

Remember that everyone's experience with depression is unique; what works for one person may not work for another. It might take some trial-and-error before finding the right combination of tools that best suit your needs during this journey towards improved mental wellness.

Organizations for Depression Support

When dealing with depression, it can be incredibly helpful to connect with others who are going through similar experiences. That's where organizations for depression support come in. These groups provide a safe and understanding space for individuals to share their thoughts, emotions, and struggles related to depression.

One such organization is the National Alliance on Mental Illness (NAMI). They offer various support programs, including peer-led support groups where individuals can find comfort in knowing they are not alone. NAMI also provides educational resources and advocacy initiatives to raise awareness about mental health issues.

Another noteworthy organization is the Depression and Bipolar Support Alliance (DBSA). They have local chapters across the United States that offer support groups facilitated by trained peers who have personal experience with mood disorders. DBSA focuses on providing hope, help, and education to improve the lives of people living with these conditions.

For those seeking online support networks, websites like Psych Central and Health Boards have active forums dedicated to discussing depression-related topics. These platforms allow individuals from all walks of life to share their stories anonymously or seek advice from others who understand what they're going through.

Remember that reaching out for help is a sign of strength rather than weakness. By connecting with these organizations or online communities, you may find solace in knowing there are people out there willing to listen and offer guidance during your journey towards healing.

Retreats

Retreats can be a powerful tool for individuals struggling with depression. These specialized getaways provide a supportive and nurturing environment where participants can take a break from their daily routine and focus on their mental well-being.

One of the main benefits of retreats is the opportunity to disconnect from the stressors of everyday life. By removing themselves from familiar triggers, individuals can gain perspective and develop new coping strategies. Retreats often offer various activities such as yoga, meditation, art therapy, and nature walks, which have been shown to reduce symptoms of depression.

Furthermore, retreats provide a sense of community and belonging. Participants have the chance to connect with others who are going through similar experiences, fostering empathy and support. This shared understanding can help combat feelings of isolation that often accompany depression.

In addition to these therapeutic elements, retreats typically prioritize self-care practices such as healthy eating, regular exercise, and quality sleep. These lifestyle factors play an important role in managing depressive symptoms and promoting overall well-being.

Retreats come in many forms: some may last just a few days while others span weeks or even months. It's essential for individuals considering attending a retreat to research different options carefully and choose one that aligns with their needs and preferences.

Participating in a depression-focused retreat offers an alternative approach to healing by providing space for personal growth, connection with others facing similar challenges, and access to holistic wellness practices without distractions from daily life responsibilities

Future of Depression Treatment and Research

As we continue to learn more about depression, researchers are constantly working towards developing better treatments and improving the overall understanding of this complex condition. The future holds promising possibilities for those struggling with depression.

One area of research that shows great potential is the field of personalized medicine. By analyzing an individual's unique genetic makeup, scientists hope to develop targeted treatments that can address specific underlying causes of depression. This could lead to more effective medications with fewer side effects.

Advancements in technology also offer new avenues for treatment and support. Telemedicine, for example, allows individuals to receive therapy from the comfort of their own homes through video calls or online platforms. Virtual reality therapy is another emerging option that has shown promise in helping individuals manage symptoms by immersing them in virtual environments designed specifically for therapeutic purposes.

Additionally, ongoing research into alternative therapies such as ketamine infusion therapy, transcranial magnetic stimulation (TMS), and deep brain stimulation (DBS) may provide additional options for those who do not respond well to traditional approaches.

In terms of prevention, early detection and intervention play a crucial role. With increased awareness surrounding mental health issues like depression, more resources can be allocated towards providing education and screening programs aimed at identifying symptoms early on.

It is important to remember that while advancements in treatment options are vital, societal attitudes towards mental health must also evolve. Reducing stigma surrounding depression will encourage open conversations and increase access to care without fear or judgment.

CHAPTER 3: BREAKING FREE FROM ANXIETY

Feeling like anxiety has a tight grip on your life? Struggling to break free from the suffocating weight of fear and panic? You're not alone. Anxiety affects millions of people worldwide, but there is hope.

In this book, we'll dive deep into understanding anxiety,

its symptoms, and how you can find freedom from its clutches. Get ready to reclaim control over your mental health journey as we explore coping strategies, seek help from professionals, and uncover related conditions that may be contributing to your anxiety.

So, take a deep breath and let's embark on this empowering journey towards being free from anxiety!

Understanding Anxiety, Fear, and Panic

Anxiety, fear, and panic - these three emotions can be overwhelming, consuming our thoughts and affecting our daily lives. But what exactly are they?

Anxiety is a natural response to stress or potential danger. It's that uneasy feeling in the pit of your stomach when faced with an uncertain situation. While fear is a normal reaction to an immediate threat or danger, panic takes it up a notch.

Symptoms of anxiety can vary from person to person but often include restlessness, irritability, excessive worry, difficulty concentrating, and trouble sleeping. These physical and emotional symptoms may seem relentless at times.

Panic attacks take the intensity of anxiety to another level. During a panic attack, you may experience shortness of breath, rapid heartbeat, sweating profusely or even feel like you're having a heart attack. It can be downright terrifying.

It's important to recognize that everyone experiences anxiety differently. Some people may have specific triggers that set off their anxious feelings while others may struggle with generalized anxiety disorder (GAD), where worries persist without any apparent reason.

By understanding this spectrum of emotions - from anxiety to fear to panic - we can start unraveling the complexities behind them and begin finding ways to cope effectively. So, let's delve deeper into identifying the causes behind these overwhelming emotions and discover strategies for breaking free from their grasp!

Symptoms of Anxiety

Anxiety can manifest in various ways, affecting both our

physical and mental well-being. It's important to recognize the signs so that we can better understand and manage this condition.

Physically, anxiety may cause symptoms such as a racing heart, shortness of breath, or even chest pain. These sensations are often accompanied by restlessness and an inability to relax. You might also experience muscle tension or headaches as your body responds to stress.

Mentally, anxiety can lead to excessive worry and fear about everyday situations. You may find it difficult to concentrate or make decisions due to intrusive thoughts that consume your mind. Sleep disturbances are common too - difficulty falling asleep or staying asleep throughout the night.

Emotionally, anxiety can trigger feelings of unease, irritability, or a sense of impending doom. It is not uncommon for individuals with anxiety to have sudden bouts of panic without any apparent reason.

Remember that everyone experiences anxiety differently; these symptoms may vary from person to person. If you're experiencing any combination of these symptoms on a regular basis and they interfere with your daily life, it's essential to seek support from healthcare professionals who can help guide you towards effective coping strategies.

Symptoms of a Panic Attack

Panic attacks are intense episodes of fear and anxiety that can be overwhelming and debilitating. They often come on suddenly and without warning, leaving individuals feeling frightened and out of control. Recognizing the symptoms of a panic attack is crucial in understanding what is happening and seeking appropriate help.

During a panic attack, people may experience physical symptoms such as rapid heartbeat, chest pain or tightness, shortness of breath, dizziness or lightheadedness. These sensations can be incredibly distressing and lead to an increased sense of panic.

In addition to the physical symptoms, there are also psychological manifestations that accompany a panic attack. Individuals may feel an impending sense of doom or dread, as if something terrible is about to happen. They might have racing thoughts or difficulty concentrating. Some people even report experiencing feelings of detachment from reality during these episodes.

It's important to note that everyone experiences panic attacks differently. While some individuals may only experience them occasionally, others may have frequent recurring episodes that significantly impact their daily lives.

If you suspect you're having a panic attack or know someone who is struggling with these symptoms regularly, it's essential to seek support from healthcare professionals who can provide guidance and treatment options tailored to your needs.

Remember: You don't have to face this alone! Reach out for help because breaking free from the grips of anxiety begins with recognizing your own strength in reaching out for support.

Identifying the Cause of Anxiety

Understanding why we experience anxiety is a crucial step towards breaking free from its grip. While it's important to remember that everyone's experience with anxiety is unique, there are some common factors that can contribute to feelings of unease and worry.

One possible cause of anxiety is genetics. Research has shown that certain individuals may be more predisposed to developing anxiety disorders due to their genetic makeup. If you have a family history of anxiety or other mental health conditions, you may be at a higher risk.

Another potential cause is traumatic experiences. Past events such as abuse, accidents, or natural disasters can leave lasting emotional scars and trigger anxious thoughts and feelings. It's essential to acknowledge these experiences and seek support in processing them.

Additionally, environmental factors play a role in contributing to anxiety. High-stress environments like demanding work situations or unstable living conditions can create chronic stress and exacerbate feelings of anxiety.

Certain medical conditions or medications can also lead to increased levels of anxiety. Conditions such as thyroid disorders or hormonal imbalances can directly impact mood regulation and induce anxious symptoms.

It's worth mentioning that sometimes the cause of anxiety isn't always clear-cut - it may stem from a combination of various factors rather than one specific event or circumstance.

By identifying what might be causing your own anxieties, you're taking an important step in gaining control over them. Remember that seeking professional help from therapists or counselors can provide valuable insights into understanding the root causes behind your anxious thoughts and behaviors.

Coping Strategies for Anxiety, Fear, and Panic

When it comes to managing anxiety, fear, and panic, there are various coping strategies that can help you regain control over your emotions. It's important to remember that what works for one person may not work for another, so it's essential to find the techniques that resonate with you.

One effective approach is practicing relaxation techniques. Deep breathing exercises can calm your body and mind during moments of heightened anxiety. Progressive muscle relaxation involves tensing and releasing different muscle groups to alleviate tension. Mindfulness meditation helps focus your attention on the present moment rather than worrying about the future or dwelling on the past.

Seeking support from friends, family members, or a therapist is also crucial when dealing with anxiety. Talking about your feelings can provide relief and perspective. Therapies like cognitive-behavioral therapy (CBT) teach valuable skills in identifying negative thought patterns and replacing them with healthier ones.

In addition to seeking professional help, self-care practices such as regular exercise, healthy eating habits, adequate sleep, and engaging in activities you enjoy can significantly impact your overall well-being. Engaging in hobbies like painting or writing allows for creative expression while providing a sense of calmness.

Remember that breaking free from anxiety takes time; be patient with yourself throughout this journey of healing. By implementing these coping strategies into your daily routine and creating a support system around you, you'll be better equipped to manage anxiety effectively.

Relaxation Techniques for Managing Anxiety

When it comes to managing anxiety, finding effective relaxation techniques can make all the difference. These techniques are designed to help calm your mind and body, allowing you to regain control over anxious thoughts and feelings. Incorporating these strategies into your daily routine can provide much-needed relief.

One powerful technique for managing anxiety is deep breathing exercises. By taking slow, deliberate breaths in through your nose and out through your mouth, you activate the body's relaxation response. This helps reduce tension and promotes a sense of calm.

Progressive muscle relaxation is another valuable tool for anxiety management. This involves tensing and then releasing different muscle groups throughout your body, helping to alleviate physical tension associated with stress and anxiety.

Mindfulness meditation is gaining popularity as an effective way to manage anxiety. By focusing on the present moment without judgment or attachment to thoughts or emotions, mindfulness allows you to cultivate awareness and acceptance of what is happening within you.

Engaging in regular physical activity has numerous benefits for mental health, including reducing symptoms of anxiety. Exercise releases endorphins that boost mood while providing an outlet for pent-up energy or stress.

Another helpful technique is practicing self-care activities like taking warm baths or showers, engaging in hobbies that bring joy or relaxation such as reading a book or listening to music. Prioritizing self-care allows you time away from stressors while fostering positive emotions.

Incorporating these relaxation techniques into your daily

routine can significantly improve coping with anxiety by promoting a calmer state of mind and reducing physiological responses associated with stress. Experiment with different strategies until you find what works best for you.

When it comes to managing anxiety, fear, and panic, seeking support and therapy can be incredibly beneficial. It's important to remember that you don't have to face these challenges alone. There are professionals out there who specialize in helping individuals overcome their mental health struggles.

Therapy can provide a safe space for you to explore your feelings and thoughts surrounding anxiety. A therapist can help you identify the root causes of your anxiety and develop coping strategies to manage it effectively. They may use various therapeutic approaches such as cognitive-behavioral therapy (CBT), which focuses on changing negative thought patterns and behaviors.

Support groups can also be a valuable resource for those dealing with anxiety. Connecting with others who share similar experiences can create a sense of community and understanding. These groups provide an opportunity to learn from one another, offer support, and exchange coping mechanisms.

If you're unsure where to find support or therapy options, start by looking into resources provided by the NHS (National Health Service). They often have information about local services available in your area specifically for anxiety-related issues.

Another option is self-referral for therapy services through organizations like IAPT (Improving Access to Psychological Therapies). This allows individuals to refer themselves directly without needing a referral from a healthcare professional.

Remember that seeking support is not a sign of weakness but rather an act of strength. Taking steps towards improving your mental health journey is something worth celebrating!

Getting Help for Anxiety, Fear, and Panic

When it comes to dealing with anxiety, fear, and panic, seeking help is an important step towards finding relief and regaining control over your mental health. Fortunately, there are various resources available to support you on your journey.

One option for finding assistance is through the National Health Service (NHS). The NHS offers a range of services specifically designed to help individuals struggling with anxiety disorders. You can start by speaking with your general practitioner (GP), who can provide guidance or refer you to specialized mental health services.

Another avenue worth exploring is therapy. Therapy can be highly effective in helping individuals understand and manage their anxiety symptoms. There are different types of therapy available, such as cognitive-behavioral therapy (CBT) or mindfulness-based stress reduction (MBSR), which focus on identifying triggers and developing coping strategies.

If you're unsure about where to find suitable therapists in your area, online directories like Psychology Today can be incredibly helpful. These platforms allow you to search for therapists based on location, expertise, and specific needs.

Remember that seeking professional help doesn't mean you're weak or incapable; it shows strength and a commitment to improving your mental well-being. With the right support system in place, overcoming anxiety becomes more achievable than ever before.

Where to Find NHS Support

Finding the right support for anxiety, fear, and panic is crucial on your journey towards healing. Fortunately, the NHS offers a range of resources to help you access the help you need.

One option for finding NHS support is through your GP. They can provide guidance and information on available services in your area. Your GP may also be able to refer you to a specialist or therapist who specializes in treating anxiety disorders.

Another avenue to explore is self-referral options. Many areas have Improving Access to Psychological Therapies (IAPT) services that allow you to refer yourself for therapy without needing a referral from your GP. These services often offer evidence-based treatments like cognitive-behavioral therapy (CBT), which can be highly effective in managing anxiety symptoms.

Additionally, online resources are becoming increasingly popular as a means of accessing mental health support. The NHS website provides helpful information about various mental health conditions, treatment options, and self-help techniques that you can try at home.

Remember that seeking support is not a sign of weakness but rather an act of self-care and empowerment. By reaching out for help, you're taking important steps towards breaking free from anxiety's grip and living a happier, healthier life.

Referring Yourself for Therapy

Referring to yourself for therapy can be a courageous and empowering step towards breaking free from anxiety, fear, and panic. Recognizing that you may need professional support is an important part of your mental health journey.

When referring yourself for therapy, it's essential to consider the different options available to you. One option is seeking help through the National Health Service (NHS). The NHS provides various mental health services that can assist you in managing anxiety effectively.

To access NHS support, start by contacting your local GP or doctor's office. They will guide you through the process of referral and recommend appropriate resources based on your needs. Remember that reaching out for assistance is not a sign of weakness but rather a sign of strength and self-care.

In addition to NHS services, there are also private therapists who specialize in treating anxiety disorders. These professionals offer flexible appointment times and specialized therapies tailored to suit your individual needs.

Remember that therapy is not a one-size-fits-all approach; finding the right therapist may take time and patience. It's crucial to find someone with whom you feel comfortable sharing your thoughts and emotions openly.

Taking control of your mental well-being by referring yourself for therapy demonstrates resilience and determination to overcome anxiety, fear, and panic. With professional help by your side, you can embark on a transformative journey towards healing and reclaiming peace in your life.

Remember: You deserve happiness, fulfillment, and freedom from the constraints of anxiety – taking this step forward shows just how strong you truly are!

Conditions Related to Anxiety, Fear, and Panic

When it comes to mental health, anxiety is not always an isolated issue. In fact, there are several conditions that can be closely related to feelings of anxiety, fear, and panic. Understanding these related conditions can provide valuable insight into your own mental health journey.

One common condition often associated with anxiety is depression. Many individuals who struggle with anxiety also experience symptoms of depression such as persistent sadness, loss of interest in activities, and changes in appetite or sleep patterns. It's important to recognize the interconnectedness of these two conditions and seek appropriate support.

Another condition that may overlap with anxiety is obsessive-compulsive disorder (OCD). OCD involves intrusive thoughts or obsessions that lead to repetitive behaviors or rituals aimed at reducing anxiety. These compulsions provide temporary relief but can exacerbate feelings of fear and panic in the long run.

post-traumatic stress disorder (PTSD) is yet another condition that frequently coexists with anxiety. Individuals who have experienced traumatic events may develop symptoms such as flashbacks, nightmares, hypervigilance, and avoidance behavior - all contributing factors to heightened levels of anxiety.

Other conditions such as social phobia (or social anxiety disorder), specific phobias (such as a fear of heights or flying), and generalized anxiety disorder (GAD) are also closely linked with feelings of fear and panic.

Understanding the connection between these related conditions can help you better navigate your mental health journey by seeking appropriate treatment tailored specifically for your needs. Remember that everyone's experiences are unique; therefore, it's essential to consult a healthcare professional for an accurate diagnosis before embarking on any treatment plan.

By acknowledging the relationship between different mental health conditions associated with anxiety, you are taking proactive steps towards breaking free from your struggles. With proper support systems in place along with evidence-based therapies targeted towards each specific condition involved— there is hope for healing and finding lasting peace within yourself.

Exploring Related Mental Health Conditions

When it comes to mental health, anxiety is just one piece of the puzzle. There are several related conditions that can coexist with anxiety or be the root cause of its symptoms. By understanding these conditions, we can gain a deeper insight into our own mental well-being and explore additional avenues for support.

One such condition is depression, which often goes hand in hand with anxiety. Feeling sad, hopeless, and lacking interest in activities you once enjoyed are common signs of depression. It's essential to recognize that seeking help for both anxiety and depression can lead to more effective treatment outcomes.

Another related condition is obsessive-compulsive disorder (OCD). People with OCD experience intrusive thoughts or obsessions that lead them to engage in repetitive behaviors or rituals as a way of alleviating their distress. These compulsions provide temporary relief but do not address the underlying causes of anxiety.

post-traumatic stress disorder (PTSD) is yet another condition closely linked to anxiety. It occurs after experiencing or witnessing a traumatic event and can manifest through flashbacks, nightmares, hypervigilance, and avoidance behavior. Understanding PTSD allows individuals to seek specialized trauma-informed therapy that focuses on healing from past traumas.

Attention-deficit/hyperactivity disorder (ADHD) may also contribute to feelings of restlessness and difficulty concentrating alongside anxiety symptoms. Addressing ADHD through medication management techniques like cognitive-behavioral therapy can improve overall mental well-being.

By exploring these related mental health conditions alongside your experience with anxiety, you open yourself up to a wider range of possibilities for finding support and tailoring your treatment plan effectively. Remember that everyone's journey is unique; what works for one person may not work for another.

Improving Your Mental Health Journey

Taking steps to improve your mental health journey is an ongoing process that requires dedication and self-care. It's important to remember that everyone's journey is unique, and what works for one person may not work for another. However, there are some general strategies that can help you along the way.

Practicing self-care should be at the top of your list. This means prioritizing activities that bring you joy and relaxation. Whether it's taking a long bath, going for a walk in nature, or indulging in a hobby you love, finding time for yourself is crucial.

Additionally, seeking professional support can greatly enhance your mental health journey. Therapists and counselors are trained to provide guidance and tools to manage anxiety effectively. They can help you identify patterns of thinking or behavior that contribute to anxiety and develop coping mechanisms.

Incorporating healthy lifestyle habits such as regular exercise, balanced nutrition, and sufficient sleep can also have a positive impact on your mental well-being. Exercise releases endorphins which boost mood while maintaining proper nutrition fuels both body and mind.

Connecting with others who understand what you're going through can provide invaluable support. Joining support groups or engaging with online communities allows you to share experiences openly without fear of judgment.

Remember that improving your mental health takes time and effort but acknowledging the progress made along the way is equally important!

Further Information and Support Resources

Remember, you are not alone in your journey to break free from anxiety. There is a wealth of information and support resources available to help you navigate through the challenges and find relief.

If you're looking for further information on anxiety, fear, and panic, there are numerous reputable websites that provide comprehensive guides, tips, and strategies to manage these conditions. These resources can offer valuable insights into understanding the root causes of anxiety and how it affects our mental health.

Additionally, seeking professional support is crucial in overcoming anxiety. The National Health Service (NHS) is an excellent place to start when looking for guidance. They have dedicated services specifically designed to help individuals struggling with anxiety disorders. You can visit their website or contact them directly for more information on where to find NHS support near you.

In addition to NHS services, self-referral options for therapy may also be available in your area. Many therapists specialize in treating anxiety-related disorders using evidence-based approaches such as cognitive-behavioral therapy (CBT). By referring yourself for therapy, you take control of your mental well-being and actively work towards breaking free from anxiety.

It's important to remember that sometimes anxiety might be a symptom of an underlying mental health condition such as depression or obsessive-compulsive disorder (OCD). Exploring related mental health conditions with the guidance of a healthcare professional can lead to better diagnosis and tailored treatment plans.

As you continue on your journey towards improved mental health, always remember that reaching out for help is a sign of strength rather than weakness. With determination, patience, and appropriate support systems in place – including relaxation techniques like deep breathing exercises or mindfulness practices – it's possible to break free from the grip of anxiety.

Take small steps each day towards managing your fears and anxieties while embracing self-care practices that nourish both mind and body. Surround yourself with positive influences who understand what you're going through – whether it's friends who lend an empathetic ear or support groups where you can share experiences and learn from others.

CHAPTER 4: THE POWER OF THE MINDSET

Unlocking the incredible potential of our minds is a journey that can lead to profound transformation and personal growth. The power of the mind is an extraordinary force, capable of shaping our reality, influencing our emotions, and even driving our success or failure in life. Yet, all too often, we underestimate its true potential.

In this book, we will delve into the fascinating world of mindset and explore how negative thinking can contribute to Self-Sabotage while exacerbating feelings of depression and anxiety. But fear not! We will also discover how harnessing the power of positive thinking can unleash a cascade of benefits for your mental well-being.

Prepare to embark on an enlightening journey as we uncover the secrets behind cultivating a positive mindset, training your mind for success, incorporating mindset into business endeavors, and ultimately unleashing the full power of your magnificent mind. So, grab a cup of tea (or coffee) and get ready to unlock your inner potential like never before!

Understanding the Power of the Mind

The human mind is a complex and extraordinary entity. It holds tremendous power to shape our lives and influence our experiences. Yet, many people underestimate just how much control their mindset has over their reality.

One fascinating aspect of the mind's power is the placebo effect. This phenomenon demonstrates how simply believing in something can have real, tangible effects on our well-being. Studies have shown that patients who are given a sugar pill but told it is a powerful medication often experience improvements in their symptoms. This highlights the role that mindset plays in healing and recovery.

Another concept related to the power of the mind is the Law of Attraction. According to this law, like attracts like – meaning that positive thoughts attract positive outcomes, while negative thoughts draw in negativity. By focusing on what we want rather than what we fear or lack, we can manifest abundance and success into our lives.

Numerous quotes from influential individuals throughout history speak to the inherent power of the mind. Albert Einstein once said, "Imagination is more important than knowledge." This statement acknowledges that creativity and vision are key drivers for innovation and progress.

Negative thinking can be detrimental not only to our overall well-being but also to achieving personal goals. When we constantly doubt ourselves or focus on potential obstacles instead of possibilities, we sabotage our own success before even giving it a chance.

Furthermore, negative thinking has been closely linked with worsening depression and anxiety symptoms. The continuous cycle of pessimistic thoughts feeds into these mental health disorders by reinforcing feelings of hopelessness and worthlessness.

Fortunately, harnessing this immense power lies within everyone's grasp through cultivating a positive mindset. By consciously choosing optimistic perspectives and reframing challenges as opportunities for growth, we can shift our energy towards positivity.

Using affirmations – short statements repeated daily – helps rewire neural pathways in favor of empowering beliefs about ourselves and our capabilities. Visualizing desired outcomes stimulates motivation by creating vivid mental images of success.

Your thoughts have the power to shape your reality.

The Placebo Effect and Mindset

When it comes to the power of the mind, one fascinating phenomenon that highlights its potential is the placebo effect. The placebo effect occurs when a person experiences positive changes in their health or well-being, despite receiving a treatment that has no active ingredients or therapeutic value.

This intriguing phenomenon demonstrates just how influential our mindset can be on our physical and mental well-being. When we believe something will work, whether it's a sugar pill or an actual medication, our minds have the ability to initiate healing processes within our bodies.

Research has shown that individuals with a positive mindset tend to experience more significant improvements from placebos than those with negative attitudes. This suggests that having an optimistic outlook can enhance the effectiveness of any treatment, even if it lacks medical benefits.

Moreover, the placebo effect underscores the importance of belief in ourselves and our abilities. Our mindset plays a crucial role in shaping our reality and influencing outcomes in various aspects of life. By harnessing this power through positive thinking and cultivating an empowering mindset, we can unlock untapped potential within ourselves.

So next time you face challenges or setbacks, remember the incredible capacity your mind holds for creating change. Embrace positivity and adopt a growth-oriented mindset – who knows what amazing transformations lie ahead?

The Law of Attraction and Mind Power

Have you ever heard of the Law of Attraction? It's a concept that suggests that like attracts like, meaning that positive or negative thoughts can bring about corresponding experiences in our lives. This idea is closely tied to the power of our mindset.

According to this law, if we have a positive mindset and focus on attracting good things into our lives, we are more likely to manifest those things. On the other hand, if we constantly dwell on negativity and believe that bad things will happen to us, we may unwittingly attract those negative experiences.

This concept may seem too good to be true for some skeptics, but there is scientific evidence supporting its validity. The Law of Attraction operates based on the power of our thoughts and emotions. When we consistently hold onto positive thoughts and feelings, it can influence our actions and decisions in ways that align with those positive intentions.

However, it's important to note that simply thinking positively won't magically solve all your problems overnight. It requires consistent effort, belief in yourself, and taking inspired action towards your goals. The Law of Attraction is not just wishful thinking; it's about aligning your mindset with your desires and actively working towards them.

By harnessing the power of your mind through practices such as visualization exercises or affirmations, you can shift your mindset from a place of lack or negativity to one focused on abundance and positivity. This shift has the potential to transform not only how you perceive yourself but also how others see you.

Remember: Your thoughts have energy; they radiate vibrations out into the universe. By consciously choosing uplifting thoughts instead of dwelling on negativity or self-doubt, you begin attracting circumstances that support your growth and happiness.

So why not give it a try? Start by becoming aware of any negative thought patterns or limiting beliefs holding you back from reaching your full potential. Replace them with empowering affirmations and visualize yourself already living the life you desire.

Quotes about the Inherent Power of the Mind

1. "The mind is everything. What you think, you become." - Buddha

Our thoughts have immense power to shape our reality. The ancient wisdom of Buddha reminds us that our minds hold the key to transforming ourselves and our lives.

2. "Whether you think you can or you think you can't, either way, you're right." - Henry Ford

Henry Ford understood that success begins in the mind. Our beliefs and mindset determine whether we will achieve greatness or remain stuck in self-doubt.

3. "You have power over your mind - not outside events. Realize this, and you will find strength." - Marcus Aurelius

Roman Emperor Marcus Aurelius recognized that true strength lies within our ability to control our thoughts and perceptions of external circumstances.

4. "The only limit to our realization of tomorrow will be our doubts of today." - Franklin D. Roosevelt

FDR's quote highlights how limiting beliefs hinder personal growth and progress towards a better future.

5. "What consumes your mind controls your life." - Unknown

This anonymous quote serves as a powerful reminder that what we focus on shapes our experiences and ultimately determines the direction of our lives.

6. "Your thoughts are incredibly powerful; choose them wisely" – Louise Hay

Renowned author Louise Hay emphasizes the importance of conscious thought selection, as it directly impacts both mental well-being and overall life satisfaction.

7. "Change your thoughts and change your world." – Norman Vincent Peale

Norman Vincent Peale's words encapsulate how shifting one's perspective can lead to profound transformations in all aspects of life.

These quotes serve as reminders that harnessing the inherent power of the mind is essential for personal growth, happiness, and success in all areas of life

The Negative Effects of Negative Thinking

Negative thinking can have a profound impact on our lives, often leading to Self-Sabotage and worsening symptoms of depression and anxiety. When we constantly dwell on negative thoughts, it becomes a vicious cycle that keeps us trapped in a state of despair.

One of the most significant effects of negative thinking is Self-Sabotage. This destructive mindset manifests through a lack of belief in oneself and an overwhelming fear of failure. It prevents us from taking risks or pursuing our goals, ultimately holding us back from reaching our full potential.

Moreover, negative thinking has been found to worsen symptoms of depression and anxiety. Constantly focusing on what could go wrong or dwelling on past failures only serves to intensify these mental health conditions. It creates a distorted perception where everything seems bleak and hopeless.

It's essential to understand that our thoughts have tremendous power over our emotions and actions. By cultivating a positive mindset, we can counteract the detrimental effects of negative thinking. Instead of dwelling on limitations and obstacles, we need to shift our focus towards possibilities and solutions.

Using the power of positive thoughts creatively allows us to reframe challenges as opportunities for growth rather than insurmountable barriers. By consistently practicing gratitude, mindfulness, and affirmations, we can train ourselves to think positively even in difficult circumstances.

Remember that your thoughts shape your reality; they have the ability to manifest themselves into tangible outcomes. So, make sure you choose your thoughts wisely because they will directly influence your experiences in life.

Incorporating techniques such as meditation or visualization can help rewire our brains for success by strengthening neural pathways associated with positivity and resilience. Training the mind takes time and effort but yields incredible benefits like increased confidence, improved problem-solving skills, enhanced creativity, better emotional well-being - just to name a few!

Business success also heavily relies on mindset. By changing how we perceive challenges or setbacks within the business realm – viewing them as opportunities for growth and learning – we can drive our businesses towards success.

Self-Sabotage and the Mindset

Self-Sabotage is a destructive behavior that often stems from our mindset. When we have a negative outlook on life, it becomes easy to fall into the trap of self-sabotaging thoughts and actions. We may doubt our abilities, constantly criticize ourselves, or fear failure so much that we unconsciously sabotage our own success.

Negative thinking patterns can lead us down a slippery slope of self-destruction. It's like having an inner critic constantly whispering doubts and insecurities into our ears. This mindset not only hampers our progress but also reinforces feelings of inadequacy and unworthiness.

When we believe deep down that we are incapable of achieving success or happiness, it becomes a self-fulfilling prophecy. Our negative mindset shapes the way we perceive situations and interpret events in our lives. Consequently, this skewed perception influences our decisions and actions in ways that hinder growth rather than promote it.

The mind has incredible power over us - both positively and

negatively. The good news is that with awareness and practice, we can shift from a self-sabotaging mindset to one that empowers us for success.

By cultivating a positive mindset through affirmations, visualization techniques, gratitude practices, and surrounding ourselves with positive influences, we can begin to reprogram our thinking patterns. These tools help us counteract the negativity bias ingrained within us by focusing on what's going well in life instead of dwelling on the negatives.

It's important to remember that changing your mindset takes time and effort; it won't happen overnight. But every small step you take towards embracing positivity will bring you closer to breaking free from the cycle of Self-Sabotage.

So let go of limiting beliefs about yourself and your potential. Embrace optimism even when faced with challenges because setbacks are opportunities for growth rather than reasons for giving up. Trust in your abilities; believe in your worthiness; know that you have the power within you to create the life you desire.

Worsening Depression and Anxiety

When it comes to the power of the mind, negative thinking can have a profound impact on our mental health. It is no secret that depression and anxiety are serious conditions that affect millions of people around the world. And unfortunately, negative thinking can exacerbate these already challenging conditions.

Negative thoughts have a way of fueling Self-Sabotage. When we constantly tell ourselves that we're not good enough or that we'll never succeed, it becomes a self-fulfilling prophecy. Our mindset determines our actions, and if our mindset is filled with negativity, it's likely to lead us down a path of self-destruction.

Furthermore, negative thinking has been shown to worsen symptoms of depression and anxiety. These conditions are characterized by distorted thoughts and irrational fears. When we allow negative thoughts to dominate our minds, they only serve to reinforce these harmful patterns.

It's important to recognize the detrimental effects of negative thinking on our mental well-being. By cultivating a more positive mindset, we can begin to break free from this cycle of negativity and find relief from depression and anxiety.

Incorporating mindfulness practices into daily life can be incredibly helpful in shifting away from negative thought patterns. Techniques such as meditation or journaling allow us to become more aware of our thoughts and challenge any negativity that arises.

Additionally, seeking professional help through therapy or counseling can provide valuable guidance in managing depression and anxiety. A trained therapist can help identify underlying causes for these conditions while also providing tools for developing healthier thought patterns.

Remember, your mind has incredible power - both positive and negative. By harnessing the power within you through cultivating positivity and seeking support when needed, you have the ability to overcome worsening depression and anxiety.

Harnessing the Power of Positive Thinking

Cultivating a Positive Mindset

A positive mindset is like a ray of sunshine breaking through the clouds on a stormy day. It has the power to transform our lives and shape our reality. But how can we cultivate this powerful mindset?

It starts with self-awareness and being mindful of our thoughts. We must become conscious of the negative thought patterns that may be holding us back. By acknowledging these thoughts, we can begin to challenge them and replace them with positive affirmations.

Another important aspect is practicing gratitude daily. Taking time each day to reflect on what we are grateful for shifts our focus from what's wrong in our lives to what's going right. This simple practice helps us see the abundance around us and fosters positivity.

Surrounding ourselves with uplifting people is also crucial in cultivating a positive mindset. The company we keep greatly influences our thoughts and beliefs. Seek out those who inspire you, support your growth, and radiate positivity.

Additionally, engaging in activities that bring joy and fulfillment plays a significant role in maintaining a positive outlook on life. Whether it's pursuing hobbies, spending time outdoors, or helping others - doing things that make us happy nourishes our soul.

Self-care should not be underestimated when it comes to cultivating positivity. Taking care of ourselves physically, mentally, and emotionally allows us to be our best selves. Prioritizing sleep, exercise, healthy eating habits, meditation - all contribute to an overall sense of well-being.

Our thoughts have incredible power. They shape our reality and can even manifest into tangible results. By harnessing the power of our thoughts, we can unlock a world of creative possibilities.

When we think creatively, we open ourselves up to new ideas and innovative solutions. Creative thinking allows us to approach challenges from different angles and find unique ways to overcome them. It encourages us to think outside the box and explore unconventional paths.

One way to tap into this creative potential is through visualization. By vividly imagining our desired outcome, we create a mental blueprint that guides our actions towards achieving it. This technique has been used by athletes, entrepreneurs, and artists alike to visualize success and bring their dreams into reality.

Another powerful tool is positive affirmations. By repeating uplifting statements about us or our goals, we reprogram our subconscious mind with empowering beliefs. This helps boost confidence, motivation, and resilience in pursuing what truly matters to us.

Additionally, journaling can be a valuable practice for unleashing creativity through thoughts on paper. Writing allows us to externalize our innermost feelings and ideas in a safe space without judgment or limitation. It enables self-reflection and introspection while also serving as a platform for brainstorming new concepts.

Incorporating mindfulness techniques such as meditation or deep breathing exercises can help quiet the mind's chatter and allow space for creative inspiration to flow freely.

By using these creative thinking techniques regularly, we train our minds to see opportunities where others may only see obstacles. We become more adaptable problem solvers who are not afraid of taking risks or exploring uncharted territories.

Remember that your thoughts are like seeds planted in fertile soil; they have the potential to grow into beautiful creations if nurtured with intentionality and belief in their power.

How to Use the Power of Thoughts

The power of thought is an incredible tool that we all possess. It's like having a superpower right at our fingertips, waiting to be unleashed. But how exactly do we tap into this power and use it to our advantage?

It's important to understand that our thoughts have the ability to shape our reality. Whatever we consistently think about will eventually manifest in some form or another. So, if you want to change your life, start by changing your thoughts.

One way to utilize the power of thoughts is through visualization. Close your eyes and vividly imagine yourself achieving your goals or living the life you desire. Feel the emotions associated with that vision - joy, excitement, fulfillment - as if it has already happened.

Affirmations are another powerful technique for harnessing the power of thoughts. Repeat positive statements about yourself and your abilities on a daily basis. For example, say "I am confident and capable" or "I attract abundance into my life." Believe these affirmations wholeheartedly and watch as they become your reality.

Another effective method is gratitude practice. Focus on what you are grateful for in your life right now and express appreciation for those things regularly. This shifts your mindset from lack and negativity to abundance and positivity.

Surround yourself with positive influences – whether it's books, podcasts, or people who uplift and inspire you. The more exposure you have to positive thinking, the easier it becomes for you to adopt a positive mindset yourself.

Remember, using the power of thoughts requires consistent effort and practice but once mastered can transform every aspect of your life! So why not take control of this amazing superpower within us?

Your Thoughts Become Your Reality

Our thoughts have a profound impact on our lives. They shape our perceptions, influence our emotions, and ultimately determine the reality we experience. It may sound like a bold statement, but it is backed by scientific research and centuries of wisdom.

When you consistently think positive thoughts, you attract positive outcomes into your life. This is not just some woo-woo concept; it's based on the Law of Attraction and the power of manifestation. When you believe in something strongly enough and visualize it with unwavering focus, the universe conspires to make it happen.

On the other hand, if you constantly dwell on negative thoughts and expect the worst outcome in every situation, that negativity becomes your reality. You create a self-fulfilling prophecy where everything seems to go wrong because that's what your mind is programmed to perceive.

It all comes down to how you train your mind. By practicing mindfulness and consciously choosing positive thoughts over negative ones, you can rewire your brain to see opportunities instead of obstacles. This doesn't mean ignoring problems or denying their existence; rather, it means approaching challenges with a solution-oriented mindset.

The power lies within your ability to control your thoughts and choose empowering beliefs. Instead of saying "I can't" or "It's too difficult," replace those limiting statements with affirmations like "I am capable" or "I embrace challenges as opportunities for growth." It may feel unnatural at first, but with consistent effort, these new thought patterns become ingrained in your subconscious mind.

Remember that each thought carries energy—positive or negative—and this energy has an impact not only on yourself but also on those around you. When you radiate positivity through your words and actions, people are naturally drawn towards you. Opportunities arise seemingly out of nowhere because others sense your confidence and belief in yourself.

So take charge of your thoughts today! Be mindful of the stories playing in your mind and consciously choose to rewrite them with positivity. Embrace the power within you!

Training the Mind for Success

The power of the mind is truly remarkable. It has the ability to shape our thoughts, emotions, and actions. When it comes to achieving success in life, training your mind becomes essential. Just like any other muscle in your body, the mind also needs exercise and conditioning.

Deepening your training is key to mastering your mind. This involves practicing mindfulness and meditation techniques regularly. By doing so, you can cultivate a greater sense of awareness and control over your thoughts.

Benefits of mind power training are plentiful. Not only does it improve focus and concentration, but it also enhances creativity and problem-solving abilities. With a well-trained mind, you become more resilient in the face of challenges.

There are various lessons and techniques that can be employed for mind power training. Visualization exercises help create mental images of desired outcomes, while positive affirmations instill belief in oneself. Additionally, setting goals with clear intentions helps direct the energy of the mind towards achieving them.

Testimonials from individuals who have harnessed their minds for success serve as inspiration for others on their own journeys towards personal growth. These stories highlight how developing a strong mindset can overcome obstacles and lead to extraordinary achievements.

Incorporating mindset into business success is crucial too! Changing one's mindset can greatly influence business outcomes by fostering innovation, resilience, and adaptability - qualities that drive success even amidst uncertainty.

Remember: The power lies within you! Unleashing the full

potential of your mind starts by understanding its intricacies –
fascinating facts about brain function reveal just how incredible
this organ truly is!

By harnessing the power of your mindset through consistent
practice and self-belief, you pave the way for personal evolution
that extends far beyond what you may have initially thought
possible.

Deepening Your Training to Master Your Mind

To truly harness the power of your mind, it is essential to go
beyond surface-level practices and dive deep into the realm of
mind power training. This goes beyond simply positive thinking
or reciting affirmations; it requires a dedicated effort to cultivate
a strong and resilient mindset.

One way to deepen your training is through meditation. By
practicing mindfulness and focusing on the present moment,
you can train your mind to be more attentive, calm, and focused.
Regular meditation sessions can help you develop mental
clarity and reduce stress levels, allowing you to better navigate
challenges that come your way.

Another powerful technique is visualization. By vividly
imagining yourself achieving your goals or overcoming
obstacles, you are essentially programming your subconscious
mind for success. Visualizing with intention and emotion
reinforces positive neural pathways in the brain, making them
more likely to manifest in reality.

Additionally, self-reflection plays a crucial role in mastering
your mind. Take time each day for introspection - examining
any negative thought patterns or limiting beliefs that may
be holding you back. Through this process of self-awareness,
you can identify areas for growth and implement changes
accordingly.

Incorporating positive habits into your daily routine is key. Whether it's engaging in physical exercise or engaging in activities that bring joy and fulfillment - these habits strengthen both body and mind. Choose activities that align with who you want to become so that they support the development of a healthy mindset.

By consistently implementing these techniques into your life while remaining open-minded about further exploration of different practices – such as journaling or energy healing –you will find yourself progressively deepening your training toward mastering the incredible power of your own mind.

Benefits of Mind Power Training

1. **Increased Focus and Concentration:** Mind power training helps you develop a laser-like focus, allowing you to concentrate deeply on the task at hand. With improved concentration, you can accomplish more in less time and with greater efficiency.

2. **Enhanced Problem-Solving Skills:** When your mind is trained to think creatively and expansively, you become better equipped to tackle complex problems. You'll be able to see multiple perspectives, generate innovative ideas, and come up with effective solutions.

3. **Improved Emotional Well-being:** Mind power training teaches you how to manage your thoughts and emotions effectively. By cultivating positive thinking patterns and letting go of negative beliefs, you'll experience greater emotional balance, reduced stress levels, and increased overall happiness.

4. **Boosted Confidence and Self-esteem:** As you harness the power of your mind through training exercises, your self-confidence naturally improves. You'll gain a deeper belief in yourself and your abilities which will empower you to take on new challenges without fear or self-doubt.

5. **Heightened Intuition:** Through mind power training techniques such as meditation or visualization exercises, you can tap into your intuition more readily. This heightened intuitive sense allows for better decision-making based on inner guidance rather than solely relying on external factors.

6. **Enhanced Memory Retention:** Mind power training includes memory enhancement techniques that improve your ability to retain information efficiently. Whether it's studying for exams or remembering important details in daily life, a well-trained mind enhances memory recall capabilities.

7. **Improved Physical Health:** Your mindset has a direct impact on physical health as well! By practicing positive thinking habits through mind power training exercises like affirmations or visualizations focused on wellness goals (such as weight loss or improving fitness), individuals have reported experiencing improved physical health outcomes over time!

Incorporating regular mind power training into our lives provides numerous benefits that positively influence various aspects of our well-being - from mental and emotional health to problem-solving abilities, confidence, intuition, and memory retention.

Lessons and Techniques for Mind Power

1. **Meditation:** One of the most powerful techniques to harness the power of your mind is through meditation. By calming the mind and focusing on the present moment, you can gain clarity and control over your thoughts.

2. **Affirmations:** Positive affirmations are a simple yet effective way to reprogram your mindset. By repeating positive statements about yourself, you can train your subconscious mind to believe in your capabilities and attract positive experiences.

3. **Visualization:** Visualizing yourself achieving success or overcoming challenges can significantly impact your mindset. When you vividly imagine yourself reaching your goals, it activates the creative powers of your mind, making them more attainable.

4. **Gratitude Practice:** Cultivating an attitude of gratitude helps shift our focus from what we lack to what we have. This practice trains our minds to see abundance in every aspect of life, leading to increased positivity and overall well-being.

5. **Self-reflection:** Taking time for self-reflection allows us to understand our thought patterns better and identify any negative beliefs that may be holding us back. It enables us to consciously choose empowering thoughts instead.

6. **Surrounding Yourself with Positivity:** The people we surround ourselves with greatly influence our mindset. Surrounding ourselves with positive individuals who uplift and inspire us can help reinforce a positive mindset.

7. **Continuous Learning:** A growth-oriented mindset requires constant learning and personal development. Engaging in activities such as reading books, attending seminars, or taking courses not only expands knowledge but also broadens perspectives.

Remember, these are just a few lessons and techniques for unlocking the power of our minds! With dedication, patience, and consistent practice, anyone can tap into their innate potential for personal growth and transformation.

Testimonials and Success Stories

Testimonials and success stories are powerful examples of the incredible impact that harnessing the power of the mind can have on our lives. These real-life accounts serve as inspiration and proof that changing our mindset can lead to extraordinary results.

One such story is that of Sarah, who battled with self-doubt and anxiety for years. Through dedicated practice and a shift in her thinking patterns, she was able to overcome her negative thoughts and develop a positive mindset. As a result, Sarah not only found inner peace but also achieved professional success beyond her wildest dreams.

Another inspiring testimonial comes from John, who struggled with depression for most of his adult life. By adopting techniques to reframe his thoughts and focus on gratitude, he experienced a remarkable transformation in his mental health. Today, John leads an empowered life filled with joy and purpose.

These stories highlight the transformative power of training the mind for success. They demonstrate how anyone can achieve their goals by shifting their perspective and embracing positivity.

It's important to remember that these testimonials are not isolated incidents; there are countless others who have experienced similar breakthroughs through cultivating a positive mindset. Their experiences show us that we all have within us the ability to tap into this innate power of the mind.

So if you find yourself grappling with negativity or feeling stuck in your personal or professional life, take comfort in these success stories. They serve as reminders that you too possess an incredible reservoir of untapped potential waiting to be unleashed through harnessing your own mind power.

Incorporating Mindset into Business Success

Your mindset plays a crucial role in determining your level of success in the business world. It's not just about having a great product or service; it's about cultivating the right mindset to navigate challenges and seize opportunities.

One way to incorporate a positive mindset into your business success is by adopting an attitude of growth and learning. Instead of viewing failures as setbacks, see them as valuable lessons that can propel you forward. Embrace challenges as opportunities for growth and development.

Another important aspect is maintaining a solution-oriented mindset. When faced with obstacles, don't dwell on the problem but focus on finding solutions instead. This proactive approach will help you overcome hurdles more effectively and keep moving towards your goals.

Additionally, developing resilience is key to thriving in the business world. Understand that setbacks are inevitable, but how you respond to them makes all the difference. Cultivate mental toughness and bounce back from adversity stronger than ever before.

Moreover, fostering an abundance mentality can also contribute to your business success. Believe that there are endless possibilities and resources available to you rather than succumbing to scarcity thinking. This outlook will open up doors for collaboration, innovation, and growth.

Surround yourself with like-minded individuals who share your passion for success. Build a supportive network of mentors, peers, or colleagues who inspire and motivate you on this journey towards achieving greatness in business.

By incorporating these mindset strategies into your entrepreneurial endeavors, you'll be well-equipped to overcome challenges with resilience while seizing new opportunities along the way – ultimately paving the path toward long-term business success!

How Changing Your Mindset Influences Business Success

The way we think and perceive the world around us has a profound impact on our success in business. The power of mindset cannot be underestimated when it comes to achieving goals and driving business growth.

When you have a positive mindset, you approach challenges with resilience and determination. Instead of seeing obstacles as roadblocks, you view them as opportunities for growth and learning. This shift in perspective allows you to overcome setbacks more easily and find innovative solutions to problems.

In addition, changing your mindset can also influence how others perceive you in the business world. When you exude confidence and positivity, people are naturally drawn to your energy and enthusiasm. This can open doors for networking opportunities, partnerships, and collaborations that can propel your business forward.

Furthermore, having a growth-oriented mindset enables you to embrace change and adapt to new circumstances quickly. In today's rapidly evolving business landscape, being flexible is crucial for staying ahead of the competition.

By adopting a mindset focused on continuous improvement, innovation becomes second nature. You become more willing to take calculated risks that can lead to breakthrough ideas or strategies that give your business a competitive edge.

Changing your mindset from one of limitations to one of possibilities sets the stage for long-term success in business. It allows you to tap into your full potential by unleashing creativity, resilience, adaptability, and an unwavering belief in yourself.

Remember: Your mind is an incredibly powerful tool - harness its power wisely!

Using Your Mindset to Drive Success

Your mindset plays a crucial role in determining your level of success. It is the driving force behind your actions and decisions, shaping your reality and influencing the outcomes you experience. By harnessing the power of your mind, you can unlock hidden potential and propel yourself towards achieving your goals.

To drive success through mindset, it is essential to cultivate a positive outlook. Embrace optimism and believe in yourself and your abilities. This positive mindset will fuel motivation, resilience, and perseverance during challenging times.

Moreover, using affirmations can help reprogram negative thought patterns into positive ones. Repeat empowering statements that reinforce desired outcomes or qualities within yourself. These affirmations act as powerful reminders of what you are capable of achieving.

Visualization is another effective tool for leveraging the power of mindset to drive success. Create vivid mental images of accomplishing your goals or living out your dreams with precision details – sights, sounds, smells - making them feel real in every sense.

Additionally, practice gratitude regularly by acknowledging all that you have achieved so far on your journey towards success. Gratitude opens up space for abundance by shifting focus from lack to abundance.

Surround yourself with like-minded individuals who share similar aspirations and attitudes towards success. Collaborate with those who inspire you to push beyond limits while providing support along the way.

By utilizing these strategies consistently and aligning them with focused action steps towards your goals, you can leverage the power of mindset effectively to drive long-lasting success in various aspects of life.

The Power of the Mind in Business

In the world of business, success often boils down to more than just having a great product or service. It's about mindset - the way we think and approach challenges. The power of the mind can play a crucial role in determining our level of success.

One key aspect is how changing your mindset influences business success. When you shift your thinking from a scarcity mentality to one of abundance, you open yourself up to new opportunities and possibilities. By focusing on what you have rather than what you lack, you attract positive outcomes and create an environment conducive to growth.

Using your mindset as a driving force for success involves tapping into the power of visualization and belief. By envisioning yourself accomplishing your goals with clarity and conviction, you send powerful signals to your subconscious mind that inspire action and propel you towards achievement.

But it's not just about wishful thinking; it's about taking inspired action too. The power of the mind allows us to develop innovative strategies, make wise decisions, and adapt quickly in an ever-changing business landscape.

Harnessing this power requires discipline and consistency in training our minds for success. Through various techniques such as meditation, affirmations, or visualization exercises tailored specifically for entrepreneurs, we can strengthen our mental muscles for improved focus, resilience, creativity, and problem-solving abilities.

Don't underestimate the impact that cultivating a positive mindset can have on both personal fulfillment and professional performance within your business endeavors. A negative outlook breeds doubt, fear, procrastination – all potential roadblocks that hinder progress.

By embracing an optimistic attitude towards challenges instead – seeing them as opportunities for growth rather than obstacles - we cultivate resilience needed in today's competitive marketplace where innovation is paramount.

The power of the mind extends beyond individual achievements too; it also influences team dynamics within organizations. A leader who understands how their thoughts shape reality can foster positivity among employees resulting in increased collaboration, supportive work environments, and ultimately, enhanced productivity.

Unleashing the Power of Your Mind

The human brain is a marvel, capable of incredible feats and endless possibilities. It holds immense power that, when harnessed and unleashed, can transform our lives in profound ways. Understanding this power is key to unlocking its full potential.

So don't limit yourself by underestimating what your mind is truly capable of achieving! Embrace its boundless potential; unleash it upon your dreams; watch as they unfold before you like magic!

Fascinating Facts about the Brain and Mind Power

The human brain is a remarkable organ, capable of incredible feats. Here are some fascinating facts that highlight the power of the mind:

1. **Neuroplasticity:** The brain has the ability to change and rewire itself throughout our lives. This concept, known as neuroplasticity, means that we have the capacity to learn new skills, form new habits, and even recover from injuries or trauma.

2. **Synaptic Connections:** A single human brain contains trillions of synapses - connections between neurons that allow for communication. These connections enable us to process information, store memories, and make decisions.

3. **Mental Imagery:** Your brain doesn't distinguish between real experiences and vividly imagined ones. This is why visualization techniques can be so powerful in harnessing the mind's potential.

4. **Mirror Neurons:** Mirror neurons are responsible for empathy

and imitation. They fire not only when we perform an action but also when we observe someone else performing it.

5. **Alpha Waves:** When your mind enters a relaxed state or during meditation, alpha waves become more prominent in your brain activity. These waves are associated with increased creativity and problem-solving abilities.

6. **Limitless Potential:** Scientists estimate that humans only use around 10% of their brain's true potential – leaving 90% untapped! Imagine what could be achieved if we could tap into this vast reservoir of untapped potential!

These intriguing facts demonstrate just how incredible our brains truly are and emphasize the immense power within each individual's mind.

The Road to Evolution Starts with Understanding
the Power of Your Mind

The human mind is an extraordinary tool that holds the key to our evolution and personal growth. Understanding its power is the first step on the road to unlocking our full potential.

Our minds have incredible capabilities. They can shape our perceptions, influence our emotions, and even impact our physical health. By harnessing this power, we can transform ourselves and create positive change in every aspect of our lives.

One fascinating fact about the brain is its ability to rewire itself through neuroplasticity. This means that we have the capacity to change and mold our thoughts, beliefs, and behaviors. With conscious effort and practice, we can break free from limiting patterns of thinking and replace them with empowering ones.

By understanding how the mind works, we gain insights into how to navigate challenges more effectively. We learn to recognize negative thought patterns that hold us back from reaching our goals. Instead of succumbing to self-doubt or fear, we can cultivate a mindset of resilience and optimism.

As we delve deeper into understanding the power of our minds, we discover new techniques for tapping into their unlimited potential. Meditation, visualization exercises, affirmations - these are just some tools at our disposal for training the mind towards success.

Perhaps most importantly, by embracing this journey of self-discovery and exploration of mind power, we open ourselves up to endless possibilities for growth and transformation. The road ahead may be challenging at times but armed with knowledge about the immense power within us; there's no limit to what we can achieve.

So let's embark on this exhilarating journey together – one where understanding the power of your mind becomes a catalyst for personal evolution like never before!

CHAPTER 5: CULTIVATING POSITIVE SELF TALK

Unlocking the power of positive self-talk can be a game-changer in our lives. Imagine having a constant cheerleader, an inner voice that supports and uplifts us no matter what challenges we face. Positive self-talk is like having our own personal motivational coach, always ready to boost our confidence, reduce stress, and improve our overall well-being.

In this book, we will explore the concept of positive self-talk, its incredible benefits, and how it can transform the way we think about ourselves and approach life's ups and downs. We'll dive into practical techniques for overcoming negative self-talk and provide real-life examples to help you incorporate positivity into your daily routine. With expert insights guiding us along the way, together let's cultivate a mindset of kindness towards ourselves through positive self-talk! So, let's get started on this empowering journey!

Understanding Positive Self Talk

What is positive self-talk? It's the language we use to communicate with ourselves, shaping our thoughts and beliefs. This inner dialogue can be either uplifting or damaging, depending on the words we choose. Positive self-talk involves speaking kindly and supportively to us, fostering a sense of self-worth and resilience.

The benefits of positive self-talk are vast. Research shows that it can enhance overall well-being by reducing stress levels, improving confidence, and increasing motivation. When we practice positive self-talk regularly, we develop a more optimistic outlook on life.

On the flip side, negative self-talk can have a detrimental impact on our mental health. Constantly berating ourselves or focusing on our perceived flaws erodes our self-esteem and contributes to feelings of anxiety and depression.

By understanding the power of positive self-talk versus negative self-talk, we gain insight into how these internal dialogues influence every aspect of our lives. Recognizing this distinction empowers us to make conscious choices about how we speak to ourselves – choosing positivity over negativity for improved emotional well-being.

What is positive self-talk?

Positive self-talk is an empowering tool that can transform the way we perceive ourselves and navigate through life's challenges. It involves consciously choosing to replace negative thoughts with positive, supportive ones. But what exactly does positive self-talk mean?

At its core, positive self-talk is the practice of speaking kindly and compassionately to oneself. It involves using affirming statements and encouraging words to uplift our spirits and build a strong sense of self-worth. Instead of berating ourselves for mistakes or shortcomings, we choose to offer understanding, forgiveness, and motivation.

By adopting positive self-talk, we create a nurturing inner dialogue that bolsters our confidence, resilience, and overall well-being. Rather than dwelling on failures or focusing on perceived flaws, we learn to reframe setbacks as opportunities for growth and see ourselves in a more compassionate light.

Essentially, positive self-talk is about treating ourselves with the same kindness and support that we would extend to a close friend or loved one facing similar circumstances. This shift in mindset allows us to cultivate a healthier relationship with ourselves while fostering positivity in every aspect of our lives.

So why is it important? The impact of positive self-talk extends far beyond mere encouragement; it has been shown to improve mental health by reducing stress levels, enhancing motivation and productivity, boosting confidence levels, strengthening resilience in the face of adversity, improving relationships both with ourselves and others - ultimately leading us towards greater happiness and fulfillment.

The Benefits of Positive Self-Talk

Positive self-talk has numerous benefits that can greatly improve our overall well-being and mindset. When we engage in positive self-talk, we are essentially rewiring our brains to focus on the good rather than dwelling on the negative aspects of ourselves or situations.

One key benefit of positive self-talk is increased confidence. By replacing negative thoughts with empowering and uplifting messages, we begin to believe in ourselves more and tackle challenges with a sense of optimism and determination.

Additionally, positive self-talk can enhance our resilience and ability to cope with stress. Instead of succumbing to self-doubt or anxiety-inducing thoughts, we can use positive affirmations to remind ourselves that we have the strength and capability to overcome any obstacles that come our way.

Moreover, practicing positive self-talk fosters a healthier relationship with oneself. It allows us to be kinder and more compassionate towards ourselves, treating ourselves as we would treat a dear friend. This leads to improved self-esteem, greater self-acceptance, and ultimately a deeper sense of fulfillment in life.

Furthermore, engaging in positive self-talk promotes an optimistic outlook on life. By focusing on the positives even during challenging times, we train our minds to see opportunities instead of roadblocks. This shift in perspective opens up new possibilities for growth and success.

In conclusion (as per instructions), cultivating positive self-talk offers countless advantages ranging from increased confidence and resilience to fostering better relationships with oneself. Incorporating this practice into our daily lives empowers us to approach life's challenges with grace while maintaining an optimistic mindset.

The impact of negative self-talk

Negative self-talk can have a profound impact on our mental and emotional well-being. When we constantly berate ourselves with negative thoughts and beliefs, it chips away at our self-esteem and erodes our confidence. This internal dialogue becomes a vicious cycle that reinforces feelings of inadequacy, self-doubt, and even depression.

One of the most significant impacts of negative self-talk is its effect on our behavior. When we consistently tell ourselves that we are not good enough or capable enough, we start to believe it. This belief then seeps into every aspect of our lives, affecting how we approach challenges, make decisions, and interact with others.

Not only does negative self-talk affect us internally, but it also has external consequences. It influences how others perceive us because when we constantly put ourselves down or express doubt in our abilities, people around us may begin to question our capabilities as well.

Additionally, negative self-talk can hinder personal growth and prevent us from reaching our full potential. It creates barriers in our minds that hold us back from taking risks or pursuing new opportunities because we convince ourselves that failure is inevitable.

It's essential to recognize the impact that negative self-talk has on our overall well-being so that we can take steps towards cultivating a more positive inner dialogue. By challenging these negative thoughts and replacing them with uplifting affirmations and supportive statements, we can gradually shift towards a mindset rooted in positivity and self-compassion.

Techniques for Overcoming Negative Self Talk

Negative self-talk can be incredibly damaging to our mental and emotional well-being. It can leave us feeling defeated, anxious, and unworthy. However, there are techniques that we can employ to overcome negative self-talk and cultivate a more positive mindset.

One effective technique is monitoring our thought patterns. Pay close attention to the thoughts that arise in your mind throughout the day. When you notice negative self-talk creeping in, consciously challenge those thoughts and replace them with positive affirmations.

Another helpful technique is treating ourselves as if we were talking to a best friend. We tend to be much kinder and more compassionate when offering advice or support to others, so why not extend that same level of kindness towards ourselves? Speak words of encouragement, understanding, and love just as you would to someone you care about deeply.

Managing stress levels is also crucial in combating negative self-talk. Stress often amplifies our inner critic's voice, making it harder for us to think positively about ourselves. Prioritize activities like exercise, meditation, or engaging hobbies that help reduce stress and promote relaxation.

Embracing a positive outlook is another powerful tool against negative self-talk. Focus on finding the silver linings in challenging situations or setbacks instead of dwelling on the negatives. Train your mind to seek out opportunities for growth and learning rather than falling into patterns of self-doubt.

Challenging negative thoughts directly is an essential technique as well. Whenever a negative thought arises, ask yourself if there is any evidence supporting it or if it's simply an unfounded assumption fueled by insecurity or fear. Often these thoughts have no basis in reality but are merely products of our own critical inner voices.

By employing these techniques consistently with patience and determination,
we can gradually shift away from harmful patterns of negative self-talk toward cultivating a more positive mindset filled with compassion, self-acceptance, and empowerment.

Remember: You deserve kindness and understanding from yourself just as much as anyone else does.

Monitoring Thought Patterns

Monitoring thought patterns is a crucial step in cultivating positive self-talk. It involves paying close attention to the thoughts that arise in our minds throughout the day and identifying any negative or unhelpful patterns that may be present.

By becoming aware of our thought patterns, we can begin to challenge and reframe them in a more positive way. This means actively questioning the validity of negative thoughts and replacing them with more empowering and uplifting ones.

One technique for monitoring thought patterns is keeping a journal or using a note-taking app to record your thoughts throughout the day. Write down any negative or self-critical thoughts that come up, along with any evidence that supports or refutes these thoughts.

Another helpful practice is mindfulness meditation. By practicing mindfulness, you develop an awareness of your thoughts without judgment. This allows you to observe your thinking patterns objectively and identify when negativity arises.

Additionally, seeking support from others can be beneficial. Sharing your experiences with trusted friends or family members can provide new perspectives on your internal dialogue and help bring awareness to any recurring negative beliefs.

Remember, monitoring thought patterns is an ongoing process that requires patience and dedication. With consistent effort, you can gradually shift towards more positive self-talk and cultivate a healthier mindset overall.

Self-Talk As If Talking to a Best Friend

Self-talk is a powerful tool that can greatly influence our thoughts, emotions, and overall well-being. One effective technique for cultivating positive self-talk is to imagine speaking to ourselves as if we were talking to a best friend.

Imagine for a moment that your best friend is going through a tough time or facing a challenging situation. How would you talk to them? You would likely offer words of encouragement, support, and reassurance. You would remind them of their strengths and capabilities. You would show empathy and understanding.

Now, turn this compassionate approach inward and start speaking to yourself in the same way. Instead of criticizing or berating yourself when faced with setbacks or failures, offer words of kindness and understanding. Remind yourself that it's okay to make mistakes and that everyone faces challenges at times.

Encourage yourself by acknowledging your efforts and progress, no matter how small they may seem. Remind yourself of your unique qualities and talents. Be gentle with yourself during difficult moments instead of being overly critical.

By adopting this mindset, you can shift from negative self-talk patterns towards more positive ones. Treating ourselves with the same compassion we extend to others can help build resilience, boost self-esteem, reduce anxiety, and improve overall mental well-being.

So the next time you catch yourself engaging in negative self-talk, try shifting gears by imagining speaking to yourself as if you were talking to your best friend – with kindness, empathy, support, and love.

Managing Stress Levels

Managing stress levels is an essential aspect of cultivating positive self-talk. When we are stressed, our thoughts tend to become more negative and critical. Therefore, finding effective ways to manage stress can greatly contribute to maintaining a positive mindset.

One way to manage stress is by incorporating relaxation techniques into your daily routine. This could include practices such as deep breathing exercises, meditation, or engaging in activities that you enjoy and find calming.

Another helpful strategy is practicing self-care. Taking care of yourself physically, mentally, and emotionally can help reduce stress levels. This may involve getting enough sleep, eating nutritious foods, exercising regularly, and carving out time for activities that bring you joy.

Additionally, it's important to identify the sources of your stress and work on managing them effectively. This might involve setting boundaries with others or prioritizing tasks to avoid feeling overwhelmed.

Incorporating regular breaks throughout your day can also

be beneficial for managing stress levels. Stepping away from stressful situations allows you to recharge and approach challenges with a clearer mind.

Remember that everyone manages stress differently so it's important to find what works best for you individually. Experimenting with different strategies until you find ones that resonate with you is key.

By actively working towards managing your overall stress levels, you create a space where positive self-talk can thrive naturally without being overshadowed by negativity or anxiety.

Embracing a Positive Outlook

Embracing a positive outlook is essential for cultivating positive self-talk. When we adopt a positive mindset, we create an environment that encourages optimism and growth. It allows us to see challenges as opportunities for learning and personal development.

One way to embrace a positive outlook is by practicing gratitude. Taking the time to appreciate the good things in our lives can shift our focus away from negativity and towards positivity. Whether it's through journaling or simply reflecting on what we are grateful for, this practice can help reframe our thoughts and cultivate a more optimistic perspective.

Another strategy is to surround ourselves with positivity. This could involve seeking out uplifting content such as books, podcasts, or inspirational quotes that resonate with us. Additionally, surrounding ourselves with supportive and encouraging people who uplift us can have a profound impact on our mindset.

Taking care of our physical well-being also contributes to embracing a positive outlook. Engaging in regular exercise releases endorphins which boost mood and overall well-being. Practicing mindfulness techniques like meditation or deep breathing exercises can help quiet negative thoughts and promote inner peace.

Adopting an attitude of curiosity and openness allows us to approach new experiences without fear or judgment. Embracing uncertainty enables personal growth and fosters resilience when faced with challenges.

By embracing a positive outlook, we create space for self-compassion, self-confidence, and ultimately foster healthier self-talk patterns.

Challenging Negative Thoughts

Challenging negative thoughts is an essential step in cultivating positive self-talk. When we allow negative thoughts to consume our minds, they have the power to dictate our emotions and actions. But by challenging these thoughts, we can regain control over our inner dialogue and shift towards a more positive mindset.

One effective way to challenge negative thoughts is by questioning their validity. Ask yourself: Is this thought based on evidence or is it simply a product of my own insecurities? Often, we find that our negative beliefs are unfounded and rooted in fear rather than reality.

Another strategy for challenging negative thoughts is reframing them. Instead of accepting a pessimistic thought at face value, try looking for alternative interpretations or perspectives. This can help you see the situation in a more balanced light and discover new possibilities.

It's also helpful to consider the consequences of holding onto negative thoughts. How does dwelling on negativity impact your well-being and relationships? Recognizing the harmful effects can motivate you to let go of those detrimental patterns.

Additionally, practicing self-compassion plays a significant role in challenging negative thoughts. Treat yourself with kindness and understanding when faced with self-criticism or doubt. Remind yourself that everyone makes mistakes and has weaknesses – it's part of being human.

Seeking support from others can be instrumental in challenging negative thinking patterns. Share your concerns with trusted friends or family members who can offer perspective, encouragement, and objective viewpoints.

By actively challenging negative thoughts instead of passively accepting them as truth, you empower yourself to cultivate positive self-talk and create lasting change in your life.

Incorporating Positive Self Talk into Daily Life

Starting the day with positive self-talk can set the tone for a more uplifting and productive day ahead. Begin by reminding yourself of your strengths, accomplishments, and goals. Affirmations such as "I am capable," or "I have the power to overcome any challenges" can help create a positive mindset.

Introducing positive self-talk into daily routines is another effective way to cultivate this practice. During tasks like exercising, cooking, or cleaning, remind yourself of how capable you are. For instance, saying "I am strong and resilient" while working out can boost motivation and confidence.

Working with the inner critic is essential in incorporating positive self-talk. Instead of letting negative thoughts take over, challenge them with kinder alternatives. For example, if you catch yourself thinking "I always mess up," rephrase it as "Mistakes happen; I learn from them and grow."

Referring to oneself in third person may sound odd at first but has been shown to be an effective technique for cultivating positive self-talk. By addressing ourselves by our names instead of using pronouns like 'me' or 'I,' we gain distance from negative emotions or thoughts that may arise.

Setting daily reminders throughout the day serves as cues for practicing positive self-talk consistently. It could be a gentle notification on your phone or sticky notes placed strategically around your work area or home environment.

Checking in with oneself regularly is crucial when incorporating positive self-talk into daily life. Take moments throughout the day to assess your thoughts and feelings objectively without judgment. This mindfulness practice allows you to recognize when negativity creeps in so that you can redirect it towards positivity.

Practicing mindfulness techniques helps us stay present and focused on cultivating positive self-talk rather than getting caught up in worries about past mistakes or future uncertainties.

Remember that incorporating positive self-talk takes time and effort—it's about rewiring our thought patterns gradually—but the benefits are well worth it. With consistent practice, you can create a more.

Starting the Day with Positive Self-Talk

Starting the day with positive self-talk sets a powerful tone for the rest of your day. Instead of waking up and immediately focusing on any negative thoughts or worries, take a few moments to intentionally cultivate positivity in your mind.

One way to start is by affirming yourself with encouraging statements. Remind yourself that you are capable, strong, and deserving of happiness. Visualize success and envision a productive and fulfilling day ahead. This practice helps shift your mindset towards positivity and boosts your confidence from the moment you wake up.

Another helpful technique is to set intentions for the day. Choose one or two specific goals or tasks that you want to accomplish and reaffirm these intentions through positive self-talk. By setting clear intentions, you give yourself direction and motivation throughout the day.

In addition to affirmations and goal-setting, starting the day with gratitude can also be beneficial. Take a moment each morning to reflect on what you are grateful for in your life - whether it's big accomplishments or small joys like having a supportive network of friends or enjoying a delicious cup of coffee in the morning.

Remember that starting each day with positive self-talk requires consistency and practice. Be patient with yourself as you develop this habit, but trust that over time it will become more natural.

By incorporating positive self-talk into your morning routine, you set yourself up for greater resilience, productivity, and overall well-being throughout the day! So why not give it a try?

Introducing Positive Self-Talk Into Daily Routines

Introducing positive self-talk into daily routines can be a powerful way to boost your overall well-being and mindset. By consciously choosing to incorporate positive affirmations and thoughts into your everyday life, you can gradually shift your internal dialogue from negative to uplifting.

One simple technique is to start the day with positive self-talk. As soon as you wake up, take a moment to set an intention or repeat empowering statements like "I am capable of handling any challenges that come my way" or "Today will be filled with joy and success." This sets a positive tone for the rest of the day.

Another effective strategy is working with your inner critic. Instead of letting it dominate your thoughts, acknowledge its presence but gently challenge its negativity. Remind yourself of past accomplishments and strengths when doubts arise, replacing self-criticism with self-compassion.

Referring to yourself in third person can also help cultivate positive self-talk. Use your own name while offering words of encouragement or praise: "You've got this, [Your Name]!" This simple shift in language can create distance from negative thoughts and foster a more supportive mindset.

Setting daily reminders throughout the day can serve as

prompts for practicing positive self-talk. Whether it's through sticky notes on your desk or smartphone alerts, these gentle nudges remind you to pause and redirect any negative thoughts towards more constructive ones.

Checking in with yourself regularly is another valuable habit. Take moments throughout the day to assess how you're feeling mentally and emotionally. If you notice any negative patterns emerging, gently replace them with affirmations or encouraging phrases that lift your spirits.

Practicing mindfulness is key for staying present in each moment and cultivating positivity within us. By focusing on our breaths or engaging our senses fully during various activities, we are less likely to dwell on negative thoughts and instead embrace the beauty around us.

Incorporating positive self-talk into daily routines requires consistency and patience; it won't happen overnight.

Working With the Inner Critic

We all have that nagging voice inside our heads, constantly pointing out our flaws and shortcomings. This is what psychologists refer to as the "inner critic." It's that internal dialogue that tells us we're not good enough, smart enough, or capable enough.

But here's the thing: your inner critic doesn't define you. It's merely a product of negative self-talk and limiting beliefs. The key is learning how to work with it rather than letting it control your thoughts and actions.

One powerful technique for dealing with the inner critic is to acknowledge its presence without giving it too much power. When those critical thoughts arise, take a moment to pause and remind yourself that they are just thoughts – they don't necessarily reflect reality.

Another strategy is to challenge those negative thoughts with evidence that contradicts them. For example, if your inner critic says you're not talented enough for a new project at work, remind yourself of past successes and accomplishments.

It can also be helpful to reframe criticism as feedback rather than personal attacks. Ask yourself what you can learn from these critical thoughts and how you can use them constructively to improve yourself or your situation.

Remember, everyone has an inner critic – even highly successful individuals who seem confident on the surface. The difference lies in how they choose to respond to their self-doubt. By working with your inner critic instead of against it, you empower yourself to grow and overcome challenges.

So next time your inner critic pipes up, take a deep breath, challenge those negative thoughts, and remind yourself of your worthiness and potential for growth!

Referring To Oneself In Third Person

Referring to oneself in third person is a powerful technique for cultivating positive self-talk. It may seem a bit unusual at first, but this practice can actually help shift our perspective and create distance from negative thoughts and emotions.

By using our own name or pronouns instead of "I" or "me," we can gain a more objective viewpoint on our thoughts and feelings. This allows us to approach ourselves with kindness, compassion, and support, as if we were talking to a trusted friend or mentor.

For example, instead of saying "I'm not good enough," we could say "John/Amy is doing their best." By externalizing the self-talk in this way, we remove some of the personal attachment and judgment that often accompanies negative thinking.

This technique also helps us challenge limiting beliefs and reframe negative situations. Instead of saying "I failed again," we might say "Sarah/Tom had a setback but will learn from it and keep moving forward."

So why does referring to oneself in third person work? Research suggests that it activates different parts of the brain involved in self-reflection and regulation. It creates psychological distance that allows for greater objectivity and emotional control.

Incorporating this practice into daily life can be as simple as using your name when speaking internally or silently asking yourself questions like "What would [your name] do in this situation?" It's important to speak kindly to yourself during these moments as you would with someone else.

Remember, referring to oneself in third person is just one tool among many for fostering positive self-talk. Give it a try! You might be surprised by how much it can shift your mindset towards nurturing growth, resilience, and confidence.

Setting Daily Reminders

Setting daily reminders is a powerful technique for incorporating positive self-talk into your daily life. By setting reminders, you create opportunities to pause and redirect your thoughts towards more positive and uplifting perspectives.

One way to set daily reminders is through the use of technology. Set alarms or notifications on your phone that prompt you to engage in positive self-talk at specific times throughout the day. Whether it's a reminder to practice gratitude, affirmations, or simply taking a moment to check in with yourself, these prompts can help keep positivity at the forefront of your mind.

Another method is using physical cues as reminders. Place sticky notes with encouraging messages in visible areas like your bathroom mirror or workspace. Each time you see these notes, take a moment to repeat the affirmations or engage in positive self-dialogue.

If you prefer a more personalized approach, consider creating a daily mantra that resonates with you. Write it down and carry it with you throughout the day as a reminder of the positive mindset you want to cultivate.

Remember that consistency is key when setting daily reminders. Make it a habit by practicing this technique every day until it becomes second nature. Over time, these small moments of intentional positivity will have a profound impact on your overall outlook and well-being.

Checking In With Oneself

Checking in with oneself is an essential practice for cultivating positive self-talk. It involves taking a moment to pause, reflect, and evaluate our thoughts, emotions, and overall well-being. This simple act of self-awareness can help us identify any negative patterns or beliefs that may be influencing our self-talk.

When we check in with ourselves, we create space to listen to our inner voice without judgment or criticism. We can ask ourselves questions like "How am I feeling right now?" or "What thoughts are running through my mind?" This allows us to gain insight into our current state of being and helps us become more aware of any negative self-talk that may be present.

By regularly checking in with ourselves, we can also monitor how certain situations or interactions affect our mood and mindset. For example, if we notice that a particular person or activity consistently triggers negative thoughts or feelings within us, we can take steps to minimize exposure to those triggers or find healthier ways to cope.

Checking in with oneself is not about dwelling on negativity but rather about acknowledging it so that we can address it effectively. It enables us to better understand the root causes behind our negative self-talk and empowers us to challenge those limiting beliefs.

Incorporating regular check-ins into our daily routine can significantly impact how we approach and engage in positive self-talk. It allows us to tune into our needs, desires, and aspirations so that we can align them with empowering affirmations and supportive thoughts.

Remembering to check in with ourselves throughout the day ensures that we stay attuned not only mentally but also emotionally and physically. Taking a few moments during lunch breaks or before bed allows us time for reflection as well as offering an opportunity for gratitude practice – acknowledging what went well during the day encourages positivity moving forward.

Checking in with oneself is an ongoing process of self-discovery and growth. By making it a habit, we cultivate greater awareness of our own internal dialogue and can actively replace negative self-talk with more supportive and empowering thoughts.

Practicing Mindfulness To Stay Present

Practicing mindfulness is a powerful tool for cultivating positive self-talk and staying present in the moment. Mindfulness involves intentionally focusing your attention on the present moment, without judgment or attachment to thoughts or emotions.

One way to practice mindfulness is by engaging in simple activities with full awareness. For example, when eating a meal, pay attention to the flavors, textures, and sensations of each bite. Notice the smells and colors of your food. By bringing your full attention to this experience, you can savor each moment and enhance your overall sense of well-being.

Another technique for practicing mindfulness is through meditation. Find a quiet space where you can sit comfortably and set aside a few minutes each day to just be still and observe your thoughts without getting caught up in them. Focus on your breath as an anchor point for returning to the present moment whenever your mind starts to wander.

Incorporating mindfulness into daily life doesn't have to be time-consuming or complicated. You can take mindful pauses throughout the day by simply pausing for a few moments to notice how you're feeling physically, emotionally, and mentally. These brief check-ins help you stay connected with yourself and prevent stress from building up unnoticed.

By practicing mindfulness regularly, you develop greater self-awareness which allows you to recognize negative thought patterns more easily. This awareness empowers you to consciously choose more positive self-talk instead of getting swept away by negative spirals of thinking.

Remember that cultivating positive self-talk takes time and effort but is worth it for improving overall well-being and mindset positivity!

Examples of Positive Self Talk

Positive self-talk is a powerful tool that can help us overcome challenges, boost our confidence, and improve our overall well-being. By consciously choosing to speak to ourselves with kindness and encouragement, we can cultivate a positive mindset and achieve greater success in various aspects of life.

When it comes to stress relief, positive self-talk can work wonders. Instead of allowing negative thoughts to consume us during stressful situations, we can replace them with reassuring statements such as "I am capable of handling this" or "I have faced tough times before and come out stronger." This shift in perspective helps us approach stress from a place of resilience rather than fear.

To boost confidence levels, positive self-talk plays a crucial role. Instead of criticizing ourselves for perceived shortcomings, we can choose affirming statements like "I am talented and capable" or "I deserve success." These words build up our belief in ourselves and increase our willingness to take risks and pursue opportunities.

In relationships, positive self-talk also has its benefits. For example, instead of constantly doubting our worthiness or questioning if others truly care about us, we can remind ourselves that we are lovable just the way we are. Affirmations like "I am worthy of love" or "My presence makes a difference in other people's lives" help us develop healthier connections with others.

Remember that these examples are just starting points – you have the power to create your own personalized positive self-talk phrases that resonate with you on an individual level. The key is to be genuine and authentic when speaking kindly to yourself so that you truly believe in what you're saying.

By incorporating positive self-talk into your daily life through consistent practice, you will gradually rewire your thought patterns towards more positivity and optimism. So go ahead – start implementing these techniques today! You'll be amazed at the transformative impact they can have on your overall well-being.

When it comes to managing stress, positive self-talk can be a powerful tool. By reframing negative thoughts and focusing on empowering statements, you can reduce anxiety and promote a sense of calm. Here are some examples of positive self-talk that can help relieve stress:

1. "I am capable of handling whatever comes my way." Remind yourself of your strength and resilience in challenging situations.

2. "I choose peace over worry." Instead of letting worries consume your mind, consciously choose to prioritize inner peace.

3. "I am in control of my reactions." Recognize that you have the power to respond calmly and rationally to stressful events.

4. "Taking care of myself is important." Prioritize self-care activities like exercise, meditation, or spending time with loved ones as ways to manage stress.

5. "This too shall pass." Remind yourself that difficult moments are temporary and focus on finding solutions instead of dwelling on problems.

6. "I am grateful for what I have." Cultivate gratitude by acknowledging the positive aspects of your life even during challenging times.

7. "I trust in my ability to overcome challenges." Believe in yourself and your capacity to navigate through obstacles successfully.

By incorporating these positive self-talk examples into your daily routine, you can effectively alleviate stress levels and cultivate a more peaceful mindset

Positive self-talk examples for boosting confidence

Positive self-talk is a powerful tool for boosting confidence and believing in oneself. By consciously choosing positive language and affirmations, individuals can reshape their mindset and build a strong foundation of self-assurance. Here are some examples of positive self-talk that can help boost confidence:

1. "I am capable of achieving anything I set my mind to." Reminding yourself of your abilities and strengths can instill a sense of belief in your capabilities.

2. "I have overcome challenges before, and I will overcome this one too." Reflecting on past triumphs helps you recognize your resilience and reinforces the notion that you are capable of handling any obstacle.

3. "I embrace failure as an opportunity for growth." Instead of seeing failures as setbacks, viewing them as valuable learning experiences promotes self-growth and encourages taking risks.

4. "I am deserving of success." Recognizing your own worthiness is essential for developing confidence in pursuing your goals.

5. "My unique qualities make me stand out from the crowd." Celebrating your individuality fosters self-acceptance, which in turn boosts confidence.

6. "I trust myself to make wise decisions." Having faith in your decision-making abilities cultivates confidence in tackling new challenges or opportunities.

7. "I am proud of who I am becoming each day." Acknowledging personal growth highlights progress made over time, reinforcing feelings of competence and self-assuredness.

Remember, practicing these positive affirmations consistently will gradually transform negative thought patterns into empowering beliefs that enhance overall confidence levels.

Positive self-talk examples for better relationships

Positive self-talk plays a crucial role in fostering better relationships with others. By adopting positive affirmations and thoughts, we can cultivate healthier interactions and build stronger connections. Here are some examples of positive self-talk that can enhance our relationships.

1. "I am open-minded and willing to listen." Reminding ourselves to be receptive and attentive when someone is speaking shows respect for their opinions and fosters meaningful conversations.

2. "I choose kindness and compassion in my interactions." By consciously choosing empathy and understanding, we create an environment of warmth, trust, and support in our relationships.

3. "I appreciate the uniqueness of others." Recognizing the value of diversity allows us to embrace different perspectives, enriching our relationships with fresh insights.

4. "I communicate effectively by expressing myself clearly." Being mindful of how we express ourselves helps avoid misunderstandings while fostering effective communication channels.

5. "I forgive easily and let go of grudges." Forgiveness frees us from carrying negative emotions that can strain relationships, allowing space for growth and reconciliation.

6. "I prioritize quality time with loved ones." Making a conscious effort to spend meaningful time together demonstrates

commitment and strengthens bonds with family members or friends.

7. "I celebrate the successes of those around me." Cultivating genuine happiness for others' achievements builds positivity within friendships or professional networks.

Remember that incorporating these positive self-talk examples into your daily life takes practice but will undoubtedly contribute to building more fulfilling relationships based on love, respect, acceptance, communication, empathy, forgiveness, celebration, and quality time spent together.

Practice Makes Perfect: Cultivating Positive Self Talk

Developing a habit of positive self-talk takes time and practice. It's not something that happens overnight, but with consistent effort, you can cultivate a more positive mindset and improve your overall well-being.

One way to practice positive self-talk is by starting the day with affirmations. Take a few moments each morning to remind yourself of your strengths and capabilities. Repeat phrases like "I am capable," "I am deserving of happiness," or "I have the power to overcome challenges." These positive affirmations set a tone for the day ahead and help shape your mindset.

Another technique is to introduce positive self-talk into your daily routines. For example, when faced with a difficult task or situation, instead of telling yourself "I can't do this," reframe it as "I will give it my best shot" or "I am capable of finding a solution." By changing how you speak to yourself in these moments, you empower yourself rather than tearing yourself down.

Managing your inner critic is also crucial in cultivating positive self-talk. When negative thoughts arise, try visualizing that critical voice as an outside entity – perhaps an overly critical friend – then respond to those thoughts as if talking to them. This approach helps create distance from the negativity and allows for more compassionate self-talk.

Referring to oneself in third person can be surprisingly effective in shifting perspective and promoting positivity. Instead of saying "I messed up," say "John (your name) made a mistake, but he'll learn from it." By using third person language, you detach emotionally from negative experiences and adopt an objective viewpoint that encourages growth.

Setting daily reminders throughout the day can help reinforce positive self-talk habits. Use post-it notes or digital reminders on your phone or computer screen with uplifting messages such as "You are enough" or "Believe in yourself." These prompts act as gentle nudges towards maintaining positivity even during challenging moments.

Expert Insights on Positive Self Talk

Experts agree that positive self-talk is a powerful tool for personal growth and well-being. Here are some valuable insights from professionals in the field:

1. Dr. Kristin Neff, a pioneering researcher in self-compassion, emphasizes the importance of treating oneself with kindness and understanding. She suggests practicing self-compassionate self-talk by speaking to yourself as you would speak to a close friend in need.

2. Psychologist Dr. Martin Seligman, known for his work on positive psychology, highlights the link between positive thinking and resilience. He advises individuals to challenge negative thoughts by asking themselves if they have any evidence supporting those thoughts or if there's an alternative explanation.

3. Life coach Tony Robbins recommends incorporating affirmations into daily routines to boost confidence and motivation. He suggests using present tense statements like "I am capable" or "I deserve success" to rewire the subconscious mind.

4. Cognitive behavioral therapist Dr. Judith Beck encourages individuals to identify their inner critic and question its validity when engaging in negative self-talk patterns.

5. Mindfulness expert Jon Kabat-Zinn stresses the importance of staying present through mindfulness practices such as meditation or deep breathing exercises, which can help interrupt negative thought patterns.

By embracing these expert insights and consistently practicing positive self-talk techniques, individuals can cultivate a healthier mindset and experience significant improvements in their overall well-being.

Further Reading and Resources on Positive Self Talk

Cultivating positive self-talk is a powerful tool for personal growth, well-being, and success. By understanding what positive self-talk is and the impact it can have on our lives, we can begin to overcome negative thought patterns and embrace a more positive outlook.

If you want to dive deeper into this topic, here are some recommended resources:

1. **"The Power of Positive Thinking"** by Norman Vincent Peale: In this classic book, Peale explores the power of optimism and positive self-talk in achieving happiness and success.

2. **"You Are a Badass"** by Jen Sincero: Sincero offers practical advice on how to overcome self-doubt and unleash your inner badass through positive affirmations and self-talk techniques.

3. **"Mind Over Mood"** by Dennis Greenberger and Christine A. Padesky: This workbook provides evidence-based strategies for overcoming negative thinking patterns using cognitive behavioral therapy (CBT) techniques.

4. **TED Talks:** There are numerous TED Talks available that explore the concept of positive self-talk from different perspectives. Some notable ones include Amy Cuddy's "Your Body Language Shapes Who You Are" and Shawn Achor's "The Happy Secret to Better Work".

5. **Online Courses or Workshops:** Consider enrolling in online courses or attending workshops that specifically focus on developing positive self-talk skills.

Remember, cultivating positive self-talk takes practice. It may feel challenging at first, but with persistence and consistency, you can shift your mindset towards greater positivity and start reaping the benefits in all areas of your life.

So go ahead - start incorporating these techniques into your daily routine today! You deserve to treat yourself with kindness, compassion, and encouragement every step of the way.

CHAPTER 6: THE IMPORTANCE OF SUPPORT

Welcome to our blog post on the importance of support! Whether you're struggling with Self-Sabotage, depression, or anxiety, having a strong support system can make all the difference in your journey towards healing and growth.

In this book, we will delve into the role of a support system and explore how it can benefit you. We'll also provide practical tips for building and sustaining your own network of support. So, let's dive in and discover why building a support system is crucial for overcoming life's challenges!

Understanding the Role of a Support System

When it comes to navigating through life's obstacles, having a support system is like having an anchor that keeps you grounded. A support system consists of individuals who provide emotional, practical, and sometimes even financial assistance during tough times. These are the people who offer a listening ear when you need to vent or lend a helping hand when you're overwhelmed.

One of the primary roles of a support system is to offer validation and understanding. They create a safe space where you can express your thoughts and feelings without fear of judgment. This validation helps validate your experiences and emotions, reminding you that what you're going through matters.

Support systems also play a crucial role in providing perspective. When we're stuck in negative thought patterns or unable to see solutions to our problems, those around us can offer fresh insights and alternative viewpoints. Their different perspectives can open up new possibilities and help us think outside the box.

Additionally, support systems serve as cheerleaders on our journey towards overcoming Self-Sabotage, depression, or anxiety. They provide encouragement and motivation when we feel discouraged or defeated. Their belief in us helps boost our confidence levels and reminds us that we have the strength within ourselves to overcome challenges.

Moreover, support systems act as accountability partners by holding us responsible for our actions or lack thereof. Sometimes Self-Sabotage creeps in because there's no external force keeping tabs on our progress; however, with supportive individuals by our side who genuinely want to see us succeed, they hold us accountable for taking proactive steps towards healing.

In summary:

- Support systems provide validation.
- They offer fresh perspectives.
- They serve as cheerleaders.
- Accountability is also one of their key roles.

Now that we understand the significance of having a strong support system let's explore how building one can benefit not only your mental well-being but also aid in overcoming Self-Sabotage tendencies

The Benefits of Having a Support System

A support system can be a lifeline when navigating the challenges of Self-Sabotage, depression, and anxiety. Having people who understand and empathize with your struggles can provide immense comfort and validation. One of the key benefits of having a support system is the emotional support it offers. When you have someone to lean on during tough times, it reduces feelings of isolation and loneliness.

Another benefit is that a strong support system provides practical help in managing daily tasks or responsibilities that may feel overwhelming when dealing with mental health issues. Whether it's helping with household chores or accompanying you to therapy sessions, having someone by your side can lighten the load.

Furthermore, a supportive network helps foster resilience and motivation. Knowing that others believe in you and are cheering for your success boosts confidence and encourages you to keep going even when things get tough.

Additionally, being part of a support system allows for shared experiences and perspective. Being able to connect with others who have gone through similar challenges can offer valuable insights, coping strategies, and encouragement based on firsthand experience.

Lastly but certainly not least, having a support system promotes overall well-being by reducing stress levels. Research has shown that social connections have a positive impact on mental health outcomes by providing emotional regulation mechanisms.

Building a Strong Support System

When it comes to overcoming Self-Sabotage, depression, and anxiety, having a strong support system can make all the difference. It provides a network of individuals who can offer guidance, understanding, and encouragement throughout your journey. But how do you go about building this essential foundation? Let's explore some effective strategies.

It's crucial to identify your existing support network. Take stock of the people in your life who have been there for you during difficult times. These could be close family members, friends, or even colleagues whom you trust and feel comfortable opening up to.

Nurturing relationships with these individuals is key. Reach out to them regularly and let them know that their presence in your life is valued. Share your challenges and victories with them so they can provide the necessary emotional support when needed.

In addition to nurturing existing relationships, it's important to connect with others who share similar interests or experiences. Joining groups or communities centered around hobbies or common struggles allows you to meet like-minded individuals who understand what you're going through on a deeper level.

Expanding your professional connections can also contribute significantly to building a robust support system. Seek opportunities within your field where you can engage with mentors or peers who can offer guidance and advice specific to your career path.

While friends and family are vital sources of support, seeking professional guidance should not be overlooked. Therapists or counselors specialize in providing effective tools and techniques for managing Self-Sabotage behaviors as well as treating depression and anxiety disorders.

To sustain an effective support system requires clear communication of needs and expectations from both parties involved. Regular check-ins allow for ongoing dialogue about what kind of help is required at any given time.

Remember that supporting others goes hand-in-hand with receiving support yourself; it's a reciprocal relationship built on trust and empathy. Be sure to give back by offering assistance whenever possible while also being open to receiving help when you need it.

Identifying Your Support Network

When it comes to building a strong support system, the first step is to identify the individuals who can provide you with the necessary support. This may include family members, close friends, or even colleagues who have proven to be reliable and understanding.

Start by reflecting on your current relationships and consider those who are consistently there for you during difficult times. These are the people who offer a listening ear, provide encouragement, and offer practical help when needed.

It's important to remember that your support network doesn't necessarily have to be large in size. Quality matters more than quantity in this case. Focus on nurturing relationships with individuals who genuinely care about your well-being and understand what you're going through.

Additionally, expanding your support network beyond existing connections can also be beneficial. Look for opportunities to connect with others who share similar interests or experiences as you. Online communities or local support groups can serve as valuable resources for finding like-minded individuals.

Don't forget about the potential of expanding your professional connections as well. Colleagues or mentors within your field may offer unique insights and guidance based on their own experiences.

Remember that seeking professional guidance is also crucial in building a comprehensive support system. Therapists, counselors, or life coaches can provide specialized assistance tailored specifically to overcoming Self-Sabotage, depression, and anxiety.

By identifying these key elements of your support network, you'll be better equipped to navigate through challenging periods knowing that there are people around you ready to lend a helping hand.

Nurture Relationships with Existing Family and Friends

Nurturing relationships with existing family and friends are essential when building a strong support system. These are the people who have known us for years, who understand our history, and who genuinely care about our well-being. They can provide valuable emotional support, guidance, and encouragement on our journey to overcome Self-Sabotage, depression, and anxiety.

To nurture these relationships, it's important to make time for regular communication and quality interactions. This could mean scheduling regular catch-up calls or planning activities together. By being present in their lives and showing genuine interest in what they're going through, we strengthen the bond of trust and create a safe space where we can lean on each other.

It's also crucial to be open and honest with our loved ones about our struggles. Sharing our experiences can help them better understand what we're going through and how they can offer their support effectively. It's okay to ask for specific types of support that would benefit us most – whether it's having someone listen without judgment or offering practical assistance when needed.

Additionally, reciprocity is key in nurturing these relationships. Just as we expect support from them during challenging times, we must also be there for them when they need us. Being able to give back strengthens the connection further while fostering a sense of mutual understanding.

Patience and understanding play pivotal roles in maintaining healthy relationships with family and friends as part of your support system. We should remember that everyone has their own challenges too; therefore, empathy goes a long way in creating an atmosphere of comfort where both parties feel heard without judgment.

By nurturing these existing relationships within your support network actively you will find yourself surrounded by people who genuinely care about your well-being every step of the way!

Connect with Others with Similar Interests

One of the most effective ways to build a strong support system is by connecting with others who share similar interests. When you find people who are passionate about the same things as you, it creates an instant bond and a sense of belonging. Whether it's through joining clubs, attending meetups, or participating in online forums, finding like-minded individuals can provide a valuable source of support.

When you connect with others who have similar interests, you gain access to a community that understands your experiences and challenges. They can offer guidance, advice, and empathy because they've been there too. Having this shared understanding can be incredibly comforting when facing Self-Sabotage, depression, or anxiety.

By engaging in activities related to your passions, whether it's art classes or sports teams or book clubs, not only do you get to indulge in something you love but also increase your chances of meeting people who share those interests. These connections can lead to meaningful friendships and supportive relationships that help combat feelings of isolation.

Connecting with others who have similar interests also opens doors for collaboration and learning opportunities. You can exchange ideas and insights while expanding your knowledge base. This constant growth fosters personal development as well as provides ongoing encouragement on your journey towards overcoming Self-Sabotage, depression,
and anxiety.

Expand Your Professional Connections

Building a strong support system involves not just relying on family and friends, but also expanding your professional connections. Having a network of individuals who understand the challenges you face in your career can be invaluable in overcoming Self-Sabotage, depression, and anxiety.

Expanding your professional connections allows you to tap into a wealth of knowledge and experience from people who have faced similar struggles. Seek out networking opportunities such as industry events, conferences, or online communities where you can connect with like-minded professionals. Engaging in conversations with others in your field can provide insights and perspectives that may help you navigate difficult situations.

Additionally, consider joining professional organizations or associations related to your industry. These groups often offer resources, mentorship programs, and networking events specifically designed to support members in their personal and professional growth. Connecting with individuals who share common interests and goals can foster a sense of belonging and provide encouragement during challenging times.

Don't underestimate the power of social media platforms for expanding your professional connections as well. LinkedIn is an excellent platform for connecting with colleagues, mentors, potential employers or clients within your industry. Joining relevant groups or participating in discussions can open doors to new opportunities while allowing you to learn from others' experiences.

Remember that building relationships takes time and effort; it's essential to approach these interactions genuinely and authentically rather than purely for self-benefit. Be proactive in reaching out to others, offering assistance when possible, attending relevant workshops or seminars - all these efforts contribute to fostering meaningful connections that can form part of your robust support system.

Expanding your professional connections extends beyond immediate family members or close friends – it encompasses engaging with peers within your field through networking events both offline (industry conferences) and online (social media), joining professional organizations/associations focused on supporting career growth ,and being proactive about seeking mentorship within the workplace are some effective ways one could begin building this network.

Seeking Professional Guidance

When it comes to building a strong support system, seeking professional guidance can be incredibly beneficial. Professionals have the knowledge and expertise to provide specialized help and support tailored to your specific needs. Whether you're dealing with Self-Sabotage, depression, or anxiety, reaching out to a trained therapist or counselor can make all the difference.

These professionals are equipped with effective strategies and techniques that can help you navigate through challenging emotions and thought patterns. They provide a safe space for you to express yourself openly without judgment. Through therapy sessions, they can guide you in gaining self-awareness, understanding underlying issues, and developing coping mechanisms.

Professional guidance also offers an objective perspective on your situation. Sometimes friends and family members may unintentionally project their own biases onto your experiences, making it difficult for them to fully understand what you're going through. A therapist or counselor provides unbiased support focused solely on helping you overcome your struggles.

Moreover, seeking professional assistance demonstrates strength rather than weakness. It takes courage to acknowledge when we need additional help beyond our immediate social circle. By investing in therapy or counseling sessions, you are prioritizing your mental health and well-being.

Remember that finding the right professional is essential for building an effective support system. Take the time to research therapists or counselors who specialize in treating Self-Sabotage, depression, or anxiety. Consider factors such as their qualifications, experience level, therapeutic approach, and compatibility with your personality.

With professional guidance added into your support network alongside family and friends who care about your well-being, you'll have a comprehensive foundation of support as you journey towards overcoming Self-Sabotage, self-doubt, and anxiety

Sustaining Your Support System

Clearly Define Your Needs and Expectations

Clearly defining your needs and expectations is crucial when it comes to building a strong support system. It's important to communicate what you require from your network in order to receive the right kind of support. This involves being honest with yourself about what you need, whether it's emotional support, practical assistance, or simply someone to listen.

By clearly expressing your expectations, you can avoid misunderstandings and ensure that your support system knows how best to help you. This might involve discussing specific actions or behaviors that would be helpful or outlining boundaries that should be respected.

Remember that everyone has different needs and expectations, so it's essential to express yours openly and respectfully. Being clear about what you need can also help others feel more confident in their ability to provide meaningful support.

In addition, regularly reassessing your needs and expectations as circumstances change is important for maintaining a healthy support system. Open communication allows for adjustments as necessary, ensuring that everyone involved feels heard and understood.

Building a strong support system requires effort from both sides – those providing the support and those receiving it. By clearly defining your needs and expectations, you set the foundation for a supportive relationship where everyone understands their role.

Regularly Communicate and Check-In

Regular communication and regular check-ins are vital aspects of maintaining a strong support system. It's not enough to simply have people in your life who care about you; you must actively engage with them on a consistent basis. Regular communication allows for the exchange of thoughts, feelings, and experiences, fostering deeper connections and understanding.

Checking in with your support network shows that you value their presence in your life. It demonstrates that you recognize the importance of their support and are willing to reciprocate it. By regularly checking in, you create an open line of communication where both parties can share updates, concerns, or simply lend an empathetic ear.

Communication doesn't always have to be serious or heavy; small gestures like sending a quick text message or making a phone call can go a long way in strengthening relationships. Sharing laughter, anecdotes, or even just discussing everyday events helps maintain positive rapport among members of your support system.

Consistency is key when it comes to regularly communicating and checking-in. Make it a habit to reach out to those who provide support for you and encourage them to do the same. Set aside dedicated time each week specifically for connecting with your loved ones - whether through phone calls, video chats, or face-to-face meetings.

Remember that effective communication involves active listening as well as expressing yourself honestly. Encourage open dialogue where everyone feels comfortable sharing their thoughts and emotions without fear of judgment or criticism.

Investing time into regular communication and check-ins ensures that everyone within your support system remains connected emotionally and mentally – supporting one another through difficult times while also celebrating achievements together.

Give and Receive Support

Giving and receiving support is a vital aspect of building a strong support system. It's not just about taking, but also about giving back to those who are there for you. When you offer support to others, it creates a sense of connection and reciprocity within your relationships.

One way to give support is by actively listening to the challenges and struggles of your loved ones. Show empathy and understanding, offering words of encouragement or simply being present in their time of need. Sometimes all someone needs are a shoulder to lean on or an ear to listen.

In return, don't be afraid to ask for help when you need it. Asking for support doesn't make you weak; it shows that you value the connection with your loved ones and trust them enough to share your vulnerabilities.

Be open and honest about what kind of help or assistance you require. This helps ensure that both parties are on the same page regarding expectations and boundaries. Communication is key in maintaining healthy relationships built on mutual support.

Remember, supporting others shouldn't drain all your energy either. Set boundaries so that you can take care of yourself while still being there for others. It's essential to find balance in giving without sacrificing your own well-being.

By giving and receiving support within your network, everyone involved benefits from strengthened bonds, increased resilience, and improved mental health outcomes. Together we can overcome Self-Sabotage, depression, anxiety - stronger than ever before!

Be Patient and Understanding

Building a strong support system requires patience and understanding. It's important to recognize that everyone in your support network is navigating their own challenges and may not always be available or able to provide the level of support you need at any given moment. This doesn't mean they don't care; it simply means they have their own limits and responsibilities.

Being patient means giving others the space and time they need without pressuring or expecting immediate responses. Understand that some people might take longer to process information or emotions, so allowing them this time can strengthen your relationship.

It's also crucial to understand that not everyone will fully grasp what you're going through. They may try their best but still fall short in truly comprehending your struggles with Self-Sabotage, depression, or anxiety. Remember that empathy is learned, and it's okay if some individuals struggle to empathize with your situation.

Similarly, being understanding involves acknowledging that people make mistakes or unintentionally say things that could hurt you. Instead of reacting negatively, try communicating openly about how certain actions impact you. Remember that no one is perfect, including yourself.

By cultivating patience and understanding within your support system, you create an environment where open communication thrives, and relationships grow stronger over time

The Journey to Overcoming Self-Sabotage, Depression, and Anxiety

The journey to overcoming Self-Sabotage, depression, and anxiety can be a challenging one. It requires courage, determination, and a strong support system to help navigate through the ups and downs. Self-sabotaging behaviors often stem from deep-rooted fears or negative beliefs about oneself. Recognizing these patterns is the first step towards breaking free.

Managing and treating depression involves a combination of therapy, medication (if necessary), and lifestyle changes. It's important to seek professional guidance to develop coping mechanisms that work best for you.

Anxiety can be overwhelming, but there are strategies that can help alleviate its impact on daily life. Deep breathing exercises, mindfulness practices, and engaging in activities that bring joy are just a few ways to manage anxiety.

Remember that everyone's journey is unique - what works for one person may not work for another. It's essential to find what resonates with you personally and tailor your approach accordingly.

Building a strong support system is crucial during this process. Surround yourself with people who uplift you, understand your struggles, and offer unconditional support. Your loved ones can provide invaluable encouragement when things get tough.

Recognizing and Addressing Self-Sabotaging Behaviors

Recognizing and addressing self-sabotaging behaviors is crucial in the journey of overcoming obstacles like depression and anxiety. Self-Sabotage can manifest in various ways, such as procrastination, negative self-talk, or engaging in destructive habits.

One way to recognize these behaviors is by becoming more self-aware. Take notice of patterns in your thoughts and actions that may be hindering your progress or causing unnecessary stress. Are you constantly doubting yourself? Do you find yourself avoiding tasks or making excuses?

Once you've identified these behaviors, it's essential to address them head-on. This could involve challenging negative beliefs and replacing them with positive affirmations. It might also mean seeking therapy or counseling to work through underlying issues contributing to the Self-Sabotage.

In addition to professional help, building a strong support system plays a vital role in addressing self-sabotaging behaviors. Surrounding yourself with individuals who uplift and encourage you can make a significant difference. Seek out friends, family members, or even online communities where you can share experiences and receive support from those who understand what you're going through.

Remember that overcoming Self-Sabotage takes time and effort. Be patient with yourself as you navigate this process of growth and change. Celebrate small victories along the way, acknowledging each step forward towards healthier habits and mindset.

By recognizing and addressing self-sabotaging behaviors with the support of others around us, we increase our chances of successfully managing depression, anxiety, and other mental health challenges that may arise on our journey toward overall well-being.

Managing and treating depression can be a complex journey, but with the support of others, it becomes more manageable. There are various strategies and techniques that individuals can explore to help alleviate symptoms of depression.

One important aspect of managing depression is seeking professional help. A qualified therapist or psychiatrist can provide guidance, offer coping mechanisms, and prescribe medication if necessary. They will work with you to develop an individualized treatment plan that suits your needs.

In addition to professional support, self-care practices play a crucial role in managing depression. Engaging in activities that bring joy and relaxation such as exercise, hobbies, or spending time outdoors can have a positive impact on mood. It's also essential to prioritize sleep hygiene by establishing consistent sleep schedules and creating a relaxing bedtime routine.

Building healthy habits around nutrition is another key component of managing depression. Consuming a balanced diet rich in fruits, vegetables, whole grains, lean proteins, and healthy fats can contribute to overall well-being.

Furthermore, social support plays an integral role in managing depressive symptoms. Connecting with loved ones who understand and empathize with your struggles creates a sense of belongingness and validation. Sharing experiences through support groups or online communities dedicated to mental health can also provide comfort knowing you're not alone in your journey.

Moreover, incorporating stress management techniques like mindfulness meditation or deep breathing exercises into daily routines helps reduce anxiety levels associated with depression.

It's important to remember that everyone's experience with

depression is unique; what works for one person may not work for another. Therefore, it's crucial to find personalized approaches tailored specifically for you under the guidance of professionals while also considering input from your support system

Coping Strategies for Anxiety

When it comes to managing anxiety, having effective coping strategies is essential. These strategies can help you navigate through challenging moments and regain a sense of control over your emotions. While everyone's experience with anxiety may differ, here are some general coping techniques that may be helpful.

Practicing deep breathing exercises can be incredibly beneficial when feelings of anxiety arise. Taking slow, deep breaths can help calm the nervous system and bring about a sense of relaxation. Additionally, engaging in regular physical exercise has been shown to reduce symptoms of anxiety by releasing endorphins and promoting overall well-being.

Another valuable coping strategy is practicing mindfulness or meditation. This involves focusing on the present moment without judgment or attachment to thoughts or worries. By cultivating mindfulness, you can learn to observe anxious thoughts without becoming overwhelmed by them.

Engaging in activities that bring you joy and provide a distraction from anxious thoughts is also important. Whether it's pursuing hobbies like painting or playing an instrument, reading a book, or spending time outdoors in nature, finding activities that bring you peace can greatly alleviate anxiety.

Social support plays a crucial role in managing anxiety as well. Connecting with loved ones who understand your struggles can provide comfort and reassurance during difficult times. Sharing your feelings with someone who empathizes not only helps validate your experiences but also offers perspective and different insights.

Self-care practices such as getting enough sleep, eating nutritious meals regularly, and setting aside time for relaxation are vital for maintaining emotional balance when dealing with anxiety.

Remember that discovering which coping strategies work best for you may take some trial-and-error; what works for one person might not work for another. It's important to listen to yourself and find techniques that resonate with you personally.

By implementing these coping strategies into your daily routine and seeking professional guidance if needed, you'll be better equipped to manage your anxiety effectively.

CHAPTER 7: PRACTICING SELF CARE

Welcome to our blog post on practicing self-care! In today's fast-paced and demanding world, it's easy for our emotional well-being to take a backseat. We often prioritize the needs of others or get caught up in the daily grind, neglecting our own mental and emotional health. But here's the truth: self-care is not selfish; it is necessary! Taking care of yourself is vital for maintaining balance, reducing stress, and fostering overall happiness.

In this book, we will delve into what self-care really means and explore its importance in promoting emotional well-being. We'll provide practical tips on how to incorporate self-care into your daily routine and offer guidance on navigating difficult times through healthy coping strategies. Additionally, we'll discuss how practicing self-care can help you thrive in all areas of life – from work to personal relationships.

So grab a cup of tea or coffee, find a cozy spot where you can relax and rejuvenate your soul as we embark on this journey together. Let's dive into the wonderful world of self-care and discover ways to prioritize ourselves amidst life's challenges!

What is Self-Care and Why is it Important?

What is self-care, you may ask? Self-care encompasses a wide range of activities and practices that prioritize our mental, emotional, and physical well-being. It involves taking intentional actions to nurture ourselves and meet our needs. While the concept of self-care has gained popularity in recent years, it actually has roots dating back centuries.

Throughout history, various cultures have recognized the importance of self-care. From ancient Greek philosophers promoting self-reflection to traditional Chinese medicine emphasizing holistic health practices, people have long understood the value of tending to one's own needs.

In today's busy world where stress levels can skyrocket and burnout is all too common, practicing self-care is more important than ever. When we neglect ourselves emotionally or physically for extended periods, it takes a toll on our overall well-being. By incorporating regular acts of self-care into our lives, we give ourselves permission to rest and recharge.

Engaging in self-care not only helps us maintain balance but also enhances our ability to cope with life's challenges. It allows us to develop resilience and build emotional strength so that when difficult times arise – as they inevitably do – we are better equipped to navigate them.

Prioritizing self-care demonstrates a commitment to honoring your worthiness as an individual deserving of love and attention. It sends a powerful message that your well-being matters just as much as anyone else's – because it does! By investing time in yourself through activities like meditation, exercise or pursuing hobbies you enjoy; you cultivate a deeper sense of connection with yourself which ultimately spills over into other areas of your life.

Self-care should never be seen as selfish or indulgent; it is an essential part of maintaining emotional balance and fostering overall happiness. So let go of any guilt or hesitation you may feel about putting yourself first at times - remember that by taking good care of yourself; you're able to show up fully for others around you too!

The History and Evolution of Self Care

The concept of self-care may seem like a trendy topic in today's world, but its roots can be traced back centuries. The idea of taking care of oneself and prioritizing personal well-being has been present in various cultures throughout history.

In ancient civilizations such as Egypt and Greece, individuals understood the importance of nurturing both the body and mind. Practices such as bathing, massage, and meditation were used to promote relaxation and overall health. Similarly, traditional Chinese medicine emphasized the balance between yin and yang energies for optimal well-being.

As time progressed, self-care took on different forms depending on societal norms and beliefs. In the Victorian era, self-care became associated with proper etiquette and grooming rituals. It was seen as a way to maintain one's social standing.

In more recent years, the concept of self-care has evolved to encompass a broader definition that includes emotional well-being. Mental health awareness movements have highlighted the importance of self-care practices such as therapy, mindfulness exercises, and stress management techniques.

Today, we live in a fast-paced world where burnout is all too common. Self-care has become even more crucial as individuals strive to find balance in their lives amidst constant technological advancements and increasing responsibilities.

By understanding the history and evolution of self-care practices across cultures and time periods, we gain insight into how this concept has always been essential for human well-being. Incorporating these lessons into our modern lives allows us to prioritize ourselves so that we can thrive mentally, emotionally, and physically.

The Relationship Between Self Care and Emotional Well-being

The relationship between self-care and emotional well-being is undeniable. When we prioritize taking care of ourselves, our emotional health thrives. Self-care involves intentionally engaging in activities that nurture our mental, emotional, and physical well-being.

Emotional well-being is essential for overall happiness and quality of life. It encompasses how we feel about ourselves, manage stress, cope with challenges, and form healthy relationships. By practicing self-care regularly, we can enhance our emotional resilience and effectively navigate life's ups and downs.

Self-care provides us with the necessary tools to manage stress effectively. Engaging in activities that bring joy, relaxation, or a sense of accomplishment helps reduce anxiety levels while promoting feelings of calmness and peace.

Moreover, self-care cultivates self-awareness by encouraging introspection and reflection on our thoughts and emotions. This increased awareness allows us to identify areas where we may need support or improvement in managing our emotional well-being.

Additionally, when we engage in consistent self-care practices such as exercise or meditation, endorphins are released which boost mood naturally. These activities also help regulate sleep patterns leading to better overall mental health.

In summary, focusing on self-care habits promotes positive emotional well-being by reducing stress levels, strengthening resilience, and fostering a greater sense of inner peace.

It plays an integral role in maintaining good mental health, and it is crucial for ensuring a balanced approach to one's overall wellness.

How to Practice Self Care

Creating a Self-Care Plan

When it comes to practicing self-care, having a plan in place can make all the difference. Creating a self-care plan allows you to prioritize your well-being and ensure that you are consistently taking steps to nurture yourself.

Start by identifying the areas of your life that require attention and care. This could include physical health, emotional well-being, relationships, hobbies, or work-life balance. Reflect on what activities or practices bring you joy and rejuvenation.

Next, set realistic goals for each area of your life. These goals should be specific, measurable, achievable, relevant, and time-bound (SMART). For example, if improving physical health is important to you, your goal might be to engage in regular exercise three times a week.

Once you have identified your goals, brainstorm strategies for achieving them. This could involve scheduling dedicated time for self-care activities such as yoga or meditation sessions or setting boundaries around work hours.

It's also important to regularly evaluate and adjust your self-care plan as needed. Life circumstances change, so it's crucial to adapt your plan accordingly.

Remember that creating a self-care plan is not about adding more stress or pressure into our lives; rather it's about carving out intentional moments of nurturing ourselves amidst life's demands.

Incorporating Self Care into Daily Routine

When it comes to self-care, consistency is key. It's not just about indulging in occasional pampering sessions or taking a day off once in a while. True self-care involves making it a part of your daily routine, nurturing yourself on a regular basis.

One simple way to incorporate self-care into your daily routine is by setting aside dedicated time for yourself each day. This could be as little as 15 minutes or as long as an hour, depending on what feels right for you. Use this time to engage in activities that bring you joy and help you relax - whether it's reading a book, practicing yoga, or taking a relaxing bath.

Another important aspect of incorporating self-care into your daily routine is prioritizing your needs. This means learning to say no when necessary and setting boundaries with others. Remember that putting yourself first isn't selfish; it's essential for your well-being.

Additionally, paying attention to your physical health is an integral part of self-care. Make sure you're getting enough sleep, eating nourishing foods, and engaging in regular exercise. Taking care of your body will have positive effects on both your physical and emotional well-being.

Don't forget the power of small acts of kindness towards yourself throughout the day. Treat yourself with compassion and speak kindly to yourself internally. Celebrate even the smallest accomplishments and give yourself credit for all that you do.

By incorporating these practices into our daily routines, we can prioritize our own well-being and create space for self-care amidst our busy lives without feeling overwhelmed!

Engaging in Emotional Self Care

Emotional self-care is an essential aspect of self-care that focuses on nurturing and supporting our emotional well-being. It involves recognizing, acknowledging, and addressing our emotions in a healthy and constructive way. Engaging in emotional self-care helps us build resilience, manage stress, and maintain overall mental wellness.

One effective way to engage in emotional self-care is through practicing mindfulness. Mindfulness allows us to be present with our emotions without judgment or criticism. Taking time each day to sit quietly, breathe deeply, and observe our thoughts and feelings can help us become more aware of our emotions and better understand their triggers.

Another important aspect of emotional self-care is expressing ourselves creatively. Whether it's through painting, writing, dancing or playing music - engaging in creative activities can provide a therapeutic outlet for processing emotions. It allows us to express ourselves authentically while also fostering a sense of joy and fulfillment.

Additionally, seeking support from loved ones or professional therapists can play a crucial role in emotional self-care. Talking openly about how we feel with someone we trust can provide validation, comfort, and guidance during challenging times.

Engaging in physical activities also contributes significantly to emotional well-being by releasing endorphins that boost mood naturally. Regular exercise not only improves physical health but also promotes positive mental states such as relaxation and happiness.

Prioritizing restful sleep is vital for maintaining emotional balance. Lack of sleep can lead to heightened stress levels which may negatively impact our ability to cope with everyday challenges effectively.

Taking the time to engage in practices that nurture our

emotional well-being enables us to develop healthier coping mechanisms while promoting overall mental wellness

Self-Care Practices for Difficult Times

During challenging and difficult times, practicing self-care becomes even more crucial. It is important to prioritize our emotional well-being and take steps to nourish ourselves, even when life feels overwhelming. Here are some self-care practices that can help us navigate through difficult times:

1. **Acknowledge and validate your emotions:** It's okay to feel a wide range of emotions during tough times. Give yourself permission to express them without judgment or guilt. Allow yourself the space to process and understand what you're experiencing.

2. **Seek support from loved ones:** Reach out to trusted friends or family members who can provide comfort, empathy, and understanding. Sharing your feelings with others can help alleviate stress and reduce feelings of isolation.

3. **Engage in activities that bring you joy:** Find solace in hobbies or activities that bring you happiness and peace of mind. Whether it's reading a book, going for a walk in nature, painting, or listening to music – do things that uplift your spirit.

4. **Practice mindfulness and relaxation techniques:** Incorporate mindfulness practices such as deep breathing exercises, meditation, or yoga into your daily routine. These techniques can help calm the mind and promote a sense of inner peace.

5. **Take care of your physical health:** Remember to prioritize your physical well-being by eating nutritious meals, getting enough sleep, staying hydrated, and engaging in regular exercise. Taking care of our bodies can have a positive impact on our overall emotional well-being.

6. **Set boundaries:** During difficult times it is essential to set

healthy boundaries with others as well as with ourselves.

Managing Difficult Emotions in a Healthy Way

When faced with difficult emotions, it's important to have healthy coping mechanisms in place. One way to manage these emotions is through self-care practices that focus on emotional well-being.

First and foremost, it's crucial to acknowledge and validate your feelings. Allow yourself the space to feel and process your emotions without judgment or criticism. Remember, it's okay to not be okay sometimes.

Next, consider engaging in activities that promote relaxation and stress reduction. This might include practicing mindfulness or meditation techniques, going for walks in nature, or indulging in hobbies that bring you joy.

Additionally, reaching out for support can make a world of difference when dealing with difficult emotions. Whether it's talking to a trusted friend or family member, seeking professional help from a therapist or counselor, or joining a support group – having someone who understands, and listens can provide immense comfort.

Taking care of your physical health can also contribute to managing difficult emotions effectively. Engaging in regular exercise helps release endorphins which boost mood while maintaining a balanced diet provides the necessary nutrients for overall well-being.

Don't underestimate the power of self-compassion during challenging times. Treat yourself with kindness and understanding as you navigate through these emotions. Practice positive self-talk and remind yourself that setbacks are part of being human.

Remember that managing difficult emotions takes time and effort; there is no one-size-fits-all approach. Explore different strategies until you find what works best for you personally.

Self-Care Strategies During Challenging Circumstances

When faced with challenging circumstances, practicing self-care becomes even more crucial. It's during these times that we need to prioritize our emotional well-being and find ways to support ourselves through the difficulties. Here are some self-care strategies that can help:

1. **Acknowledge your emotions:** Allow yourself to feel whatever emotions arise without judgment or resistance. Give yourself permission to cry, vent, or express your frustrations in a healthy way.

2. **Seek support:** Reach out to trusted friends or family members who can offer a listening ear or words of encouragement. Sometimes, simply talking about our challenges can provide much-needed relief and perspective.

3. **Engage in calming activities:** Find activities that bring you peace and relaxation, such as meditation, deep breathing exercises, yoga, or taking a soothing bath. These practices can help reduce stress and promote a sense of calm.

4. **Take breaks when needed:** Recognize when you need time for yourself and don't hesitate to take breaks from responsibilities if possible. Whether it's going for a walk outside or enjoying a hobby you love, allowing yourself moments of respite is essential.

5. **Practice self-compassion:** Be gentle with yourself during difficult times and remind yourself that it's okay not to have all the answers right away. Treat yourself with kindness

and understanding as you navigate through challenging circumstances.

Remember, everyone's journey is unique but finding what works best for you is key when it comes to practicing self-care during challenging times. By prioritizing your well-being and implementing these strategies into your routine, you'll be better equipped to manage difficult circumstances while maintaining emotional balance

Thriving Through Self Care

Developing a mindful and compassionate mindset is key to thriving through self-care. By practicing self-awareness and being present in the moment, we can better understand our emotions and needs. This allows us to prioritize self-care and make choices that align with our well-being.

Utilizing self-care can help us thrive in various areas of life. When we take time for ourselves, we replenish our energy reserves, allowing us to show up fully in our relationships, work, and other responsibilities. It's like putting on your own oxygen mask before assisting others - taking care of ourselves enables us to be more effective and supportive.

Self-care is not just about bubble baths or indulgent treats; it's about nourishing our minds, bodies, and spirits. Engaging in activities that bring joy or fulfillment can boost our mood and overall satisfaction with life. Whether it's pursuing a hobby, spending time outdoors, or connecting with loved ones, these moments of self-care contribute to a greater sense of well-being.

Incorporating mindfulness practices into our daily routines can also support thriving through self-care. Mindfulness involves bringing attention to the present moment without judgment. This practice helps reduce stress levels by grounding us in the here-and-now instead of getting caught up in worries about the past or future.

Remember that every person's journey towards thriving through self-care will look different. What works for one person may not work for another. It's essential to listen to your own needs and experiment with different strategies until you find what resonates most deeply with you.

By prioritizing self-care and nurturing ourselves holistically – mind,body,and spirit – we create an environment conducive to growth, taking proactive steps toward reaching our full potential.

Whatever combination of relaxation techniques,self-exploration activities,and healthy habits you choose, may they serve as stepping stones toward fulfilling life!

Developing a Mindful and Compassionate Mindset

In today's fast-paced world, it can be easy to get caught up in the hustle and bustle of daily life. However, taking the time to develop a mindful and compassionate mindset is crucial for our overall well-being.

Mindfulness allows us to be fully present in the moment, without judgment or attachment. By practicing mindfulness, we can cultivate an awareness of our thoughts, feelings, and sensations as they arise. This heightened awareness enables us to respond to situations with clarity and intention rather than reacting impulsively.

Compassion goes hand-in-hand with mindfulness. It involves cultivating kindness towards us and others. When we approach ourselves with compassion, we are more forgiving of our mistakes and shortcomings. Similarly, when we extend compassion towards others, we foster empathy and understanding.

Developing a mindful and compassionate mindset takes practice but yields incredible benefits. It helps reduce stress levels by allowing us to let go of worries about the past or future. It also enhances our relationships by fostering deeper connections based on empathy and kindness.

To cultivate this mindset, start by incorporating simple practices into your daily routine. Set aside a few minutes each day for meditation or deep breathing exercises that help bring you into the present moment. Practice self-compassion by speaking kindly to yourself internally and acknowledging your strengths instead of focusing on perceived flaws.

Engage in acts of kindness towards others regularly – even small gestures like holding the door open for someone or offering a kind word can make a difference.

By developing a mindful and compassionate mindset, you not only improve your own well-being but also contribute positively to those around you. So, take some time each day to nurture these qualities within yourself – it will have ripple effects far beyond what you might imagine!

Utilizing Self Care to Thrive in Various Areas of Life

Self-care is not limited to just one aspect of our lives. It extends beyond the realm of physical health and can be applied to various areas, allowing us to thrive in all aspects of life. Whether it's our relationships, career, or personal development, self-care plays a crucial role in enhancing our well-being.

In relationships, practicing self-care allows us to show up as our best selves. By taking time for us and nurturing our own needs and desires, we are able to cultivate healthier connections with others. This means setting boundaries when needed, communicating effectively, and prioritizing quality time with loved ones.

When it comes to careers and professional growth, self-care is essential for maintaining a healthy work-life balance. Taking breaks throughout the day, setting realistic goals and expectations for ourselves, and finding ways to manage stress can greatly contribute to overall job satisfaction and success.

Additionally, self-care helps foster personal development by allowing us the space for introspection and growth. Engaging in activities that bring joy or learning new skills not only boosts confidence but also provides a sense of fulfillment outside of external pressures.

By incorporating self-care practices into these different areas of life - relationships, career, personal development - we are able to create a holistic approach that promotes overall well-being. So, remember prioritizing yourself! Your happiness and thriving in all areas depend on it!

Self-Care at Work

In today's fast-paced and demanding work environments, practicing self-care is crucial for maintaining emotional well-being. Taking care of yourself not only benefits your own mental health but also enhances productivity and job satisfaction. Implementing self-care habits in the workplace can help create a positive and supportive atmosphere.

One way to prioritize self-care at work is by setting boundaries. Establish clear expectations with your colleagues and superiors about your availability outside of working hours. Avoid constantly checking emails or taking on additional tasks that can lead to burnout.

Another important aspect of self-care at work is finding balance between professional responsibilities and personal life. Make time for activities that bring you joy outside of work, whether it's exercising, spending time with loved ones, or pursuing hobbies. Remember that a healthy work-life balance contributes to overall well-being.

Taking regular breaks throughout the day is another effective strategy for practicing self-care at work. Step away from your desk, stretch, or engage in deep breathing exercises to recharge both physically and mentally. This helps prevent exhaustion and promotes focus when returning to tasks.

Additionally, creating a positive workspace can significantly impact your emotional well-being. Personalize your desk area with items that bring you comfort or inspiration - such as plants, photos, or motivational quotes. Surrounding yourself with uplifting elements can contribute to a more pleasant working environment.

Don't be afraid to ask for support when needed. Reach out to trusted colleagues or supervisors if you're feeling overwhelmed or stressed. Seeking assistance shows strength rather than weakness and allows others the opportunity to provide guidance or resources.

By prioritizing self-care in the workplace, you are investing in your overall happiness and success both professionally and personally.

Implementing Self Care Habits in the Workplace

In today's fast-paced and often stressful work environments, it is essential to prioritize self-care. Taking care of ourselves not only benefits our overall well-being but also enhances our productivity and performance at work. Implementing self-care habits in the workplace can help create a healthier and more positive work environment.

One important aspect of implementing self-care habits is setting boundaries. It's crucial to establish clear boundaries between work and personal life, ensuring that you have time for relaxation, hobbies, and spending quality time with loved ones. This allows you to recharge your batteries outside of work hours and prevents burnout.

Another key element is practicing stress management techniques during the workday. This can include deep breathing exercises, taking short breaks throughout the day, or engaging in mindfulness practices. These strategies help reduce stress levels and promote mental clarity.

Additionally, fostering a supportive workplace culture that encourages open communication and collaboration can contribute to overall employee well-being. When employees feel supported by their colleagues and superiors, they are more likely to experience higher job satisfaction and lower levels of stress.

Engaging in physical activity during the workday can also

be beneficial for both physical health and emotional well-being. Whether it's going for a walk during lunch break or incorporating stretching exercises at your desk, moving your body helps release tension and boosts mood.

Promoting self-care resources within the workplace such as access to mental health services or wellness programs can further support employees' well-being journey. Companies can provide workshops on topics like stress management or offer flexible schedules that allow employees to attend appointments or engage in self-care activities without feeling guilty.

By implementing these self-care habits into the workplace routine, organizations can create an environment where employees feel valued as individuals with unique needs for balance between their personal lives and professional responsibilities.

Finding Balance Between Work and Personal Life

Finding balance between work and personal life is essential for maintaining overall well-being. In today's fast-paced world, it can be challenging to find the right equilibrium, but it is crucial for our emotional health.

One way to achieve this balance is by setting boundaries. Clearly defining your working hours and sticking to them allows you to prioritize your personal life without feeling guilty or overwhelmed. It also helps prevent burnout and ensures that you have time for self-care activities.

Another helpful strategy is learning how to delegate tasks effectively. If possible, try to share responsibilities with colleagues or outsource certain tasks so that you don't feel overwhelmed with a heavy workload. This will free up more time for yourself outside of work.

Additionally, make sure to schedule regular breaks throughout the day and take time off when needed. Allowing yourself moments of rest and relaxation can help recharge your energy levels and improve productivity in the long run.

It's also important to create clear distinctions between work and personal spaces. Designate specific areas in your home for work-related activities, if possible, separate from where you relax or spend quality time with loved ones.

Remember that finding balance requires ongoing evaluation and adjustment as priorities shift over time. Be flexible and willing to adapt as needed while always keeping your well-being at the forefront.

By prioritizing a healthy balance between work obligations and personal life commitments, you can cultivate a greater sense of fulfillment both professionally and personally—leading ultimately leading towards increased happiness overall.

Read More for Additional Self Care Resources and Inspiration

Practicing self-care is not a one-time task, but rather an ongoing journey. It requires dedication and commitment to prioritize your own well-being. Remember, you deserve to care for yourself just as much as you care for others.

If you're looking for more guidance on self-care or seeking additional resources and inspiration, here are some suggestions:

1. **Books:** Explore the world of self-help books that focus on various aspects of self-care such as mental health, mindfulness, meditation, and personal development. Some popular titles include "The Gifts of Imperfection" by Brené Brown, "The Four Agreements" by Don Miguel Ruiz, and "Atomic Habits" by James Clear.

2. **Online Communities:** Join online communities or forums where individuals share their experiences with self-care practices. These platforms serve as a supportive space to learn from others' journeys and find inspiration in their stories.

3. **Podcasts:** Tune in to podcasts that discuss topics related to emotional well-being and self-improvement. Some notable podcasts include "The Life Coach School Podcast" hosted by Brooke Castillo," The Tony Robbins Podcast," and "The School of Greatness" hosted by Lewis Howes.

4. **Workshops/Retreats:** Consider attending workshops or retreats focused on personal growth and healing. These immersive experiences provide opportunities to deepen your understanding of self-care techniques while connecting with like-minded individuals.

5. **Therapist/Counselor:** If you're struggling with managing your emotions or finding it challenging to practice self-care

independently, consider reaching out to a therapist or counselor who can guide you through the process.

Remember that practicing self-care is a highly individualized journey – what works for someone else may not work for you! Be open-minded in exploring different approaches until you find what resonates best with your needs and preferences.

By prioritizing yourself through regular acts of kindness, setting boundaries, and engaging in activities that bring you joy and peace, you can cultivate

CHAPTER 8: FOSTERING RESILIENCE

Resilience is the secret ingredient to living a fulfilling and successful life. It allows us to navigate through obstacles, adapt to change, and bounce back from setbacks with unwavering determination. By fostering resilience within us, we can break free from unnecessary limitations that hold us back from reaching our true potential.

So how do we cultivate resilience? It starts with understanding that challenges are an inevitable part of life. Instead of viewing them as roadblocks, we can choose to see them as opportunities for growth and learning. Embracing a mindset of resilience means shifting our perspective and reframing difficulties as stepping stones towards personal development.

Practicing self-care is another essential aspect of building resilience. Taking care of our physical, mental, and emotional well-being lays a strong foundation for navigating challenges effectively. This might involve taking regular breaks, engaging in activities that bring joy and relaxation, seeking support from loved ones or professionals when needed, and prioritizing self-reflection and introspection.

Building a network of positive relationships also plays a crucial role in fostering resilience. Surrounding ourselves with individuals who uplift and inspire us creates an environment where we feel supported during tough times. These connections provide encouragement, guidance, and empathy when we need it most.

Another key element in developing resilience is setting realistic goals. By breaking down big aspirations into smaller achievable steps, we create momentum that keeps us motivated even when faced with obstacles along the way. Setting attainable targets helps build confidence in our abilities while allowing room for adjustment if necessary.

Lastly but certainly not least important is embracing failure as a valuable teacher on the journey towards resilience. Failure isn't something to be feared or avoided; instead, it provides valuable lessons that help shape our character and strengthen our resolve. Viewing failure through this lens allows us to bounce back stronger than before by learning from past mistakes rather than dwelling on them.

By embracing these strategies for cultivating resilience within ourselves, we can begin thriving without unnecessary limitations. Life may throw curveballs our way, but with resilience as our ally

The Essence of Resilience

Resilience is the essence of our ability to bounce back from life's challenges and setbacks. It is the inner strength that allows us to adapt, grow, and thrive in the face of adversity. Resilience is not about avoiding difficulties or pretending that everything is fine; it's about facing them head-on and finding ways to overcome them.

At its core, resilience involves developing a positive mindset, cultivating self-compassion, and building strong support networks. It requires embracing change as an opportunity for growth rather than fearing it as a threat.

Resilience is not something we are born with; it can be learned and developed over time. By practicing mindfulness and staying connected to our emotions, we can better understand ourselves and build resilience. This means acknowledging our feelings without judgment or criticism.

One way to foster resilience is by setting realistic goals for ourselves. By breaking big challenges into smaller manageable steps, we can build confidence in our ability to overcome obstacles.

Another important aspect of resilience is maintaining positive relationships with others. Surrounding ourselves with supportive friends, family members, or mentors can provide a sense of belonging and reinforce our belief in ourselves.

Embracing resilience allows us to navigate life's ups and downs with greater ease. It empowers us to keep moving forward even when faced with adversity. So, let's embrace the power of resilience today!

Practicing Your Resilience

Resilience is not something that magically appears overnight. It's a skill that can be honed and cultivated through practice and perseverance. So, how exactly do you practice resilience?

It's important to recognize that resilience is not about avoiding or ignoring challenges; it's about facing them head-on with determination and adaptability. One way to practice resilience is by reframing setbacks as opportunities for growth and learning. Instead of dwelling on what went wrong, focus on what you can learn from the experience.

Another effective strategy is building a strong support network. Surround yourself with positive influences who uplift and encourage you during difficult times. Seek out mentors or role models who have overcome obstacles similar to yours, and learn from their experiences.

Additionally, taking care of your physical and mental well-being can greatly enhance your ability to bounce back from adversity. Exercise regularly, eat nutritious meals, get enough sleep, and engage in activities that bring you joy.

Developing a growth mindset can significantly boost your resilience levels. Embrace challenges as opportunities for personal development rather than viewing them as threats or failures.

Remember, practicing resilience takes time and effort but the rewards are worth it! By actively working on strengthening your ability to bounce back from setbacks, you will become more resilient in all areas of life.

5 Ways to Build Resilience

Building resilience is essential for navigating life's challenges and setbacks. It allows us to bounce back stronger and continue moving forward. Here are five effective ways to cultivate resilience:

1. **Take Full Days Off:** Giving yourself regular breaks from work or responsibilities is crucial for mental and emotional rejuvenation. Use this time to engage in activities that bring you joy, whether it's spending time with loved ones, pursuing a hobby, or simply resting.

2. **Meditate Daily (or as often as possible):** Meditation has been proven to reduce stress levels and improve overall well-being. By taking a few moments each day to quiet your mind and focus on the present moment, you can develop inner strength and clarity.

3. **Use Affirmations to Fortify Your Resilience:** Positive affirmations help reframe negative thoughts into empowering beliefs. Repeat statements like "I am capable of overcoming any challenge" or "I embrace change with confidence" regularly to reinforce your resilience mindset.

4. **Reawaken Your Spiritual Practices:** Connecting with something greater than ourselves can provide solace during difficult times. Whether through prayer, meditation, or engaging in nature, nurturing your spirituality can offer comfort and guidance when facing adversity.

5. **Seek Support from Trusted Individuals:** Building a strong support network is vital for resilience-building. Reach out to family members, friends, or mentors who can offer encouragement and perspective during challenging times.

By incorporating these practices into our lives consistently, we can enhance our ability to bounce back from obstacles while fostering personal growth along the way.

Monitoring Our Well-Being

Taking care of our well-being is crucial for living a fulfilling and resilient life. It's important to pay attention to our physical, mental, and emotional health on a regular basis. But how can we effectively monitor our well-being?

It's essential to listen to our bodies and notice any signs of stress or fatigue. This means being aware of how we feel physically – are we experiencing any pain or discomfort? Are we getting enough sleep and eating nutritious food? By tuning into these bodily cues, we can make necessary adjustments to support our overall well-being.

Monitoring our mental and emotional health involves paying attention to our thoughts and feelings. Are there any negative thought patterns that keep recurring? How do certain situations or relationships impact our mood? Taking the time for self-reflection allows us to identify areas where we may need additional support or healing.

Additionally, seeking feedback from trusted friends or professionals can provide valuable insights into areas where we might be overlooking self-care. Sometimes an outside perspective can shed light on blind spots that hinder our well-being.

Monitoring our well-being requires ongoing attentiveness and self-awareness. It's about recognizing when something feels off and taking proactive steps towards improving ourselves holistically. By prioritizing this practice in our daily lives, we embrace resilience by ensuring that both physical and mental aspects of ourselves are nurtured with love and care.

Suicide Prevention is a topic that deserves our utmost attention and care. It's a difficult subject to discuss, but it's crucial that we break the silence and create a supportive environment for those who may be struggling. By fostering resilience and providing resources, we can help individuals navigate through their darkest moments.

Education plays a vital role in suicide prevention. We need to ensure that people are aware of the warning signs and risk factors associated with suicide. This knowledge empowers us to recognize when someone might be in crisis and intervene before it's too late.

Support networks are also essential in preventing suicide. Creating spaces where individuals feel safe to open up about their struggles without fear of judgment or stigma is crucial. Encouraging open conversations about mental health helps reduce feelings of isolation and provides an avenue for seeking help.

Accessing professional support is another vital aspect of suicide prevention. Mental health professionals can offer guidance, therapy, and treatment options tailored to each individual's needs. Additionally, helplines and crisis intervention services provide immediate assistance when someone feels overwhelmed.

Promoting self-care practices such as exercise, mindfulness techniques like meditation or yoga, maintaining healthy relationships, and engaging in hobbies can contribute significantly to overall well-being.

Let us continue working together towards creating a world where no one has to suffer alone or feel trapped by despair. Together we can make a difference by embracing resilience and supporting one another on this journey called life.

Teaching resilience to children is a crucial aspect of their overall development. Resilience allows them to navigate through life's challenges with confidence and adaptability. It helps build their mental and emotional strength, enabling them to bounce back from setbacks and persevere in the face of adversity.

One effective way to teach resilience to children is by encouraging them to embrace failure as a learning opportunity rather than a defeat. By reframing failures as stepping stones towards success, we can help them develop a growth mindset that fosters resilience.

Another important aspect is teaching children problem-solving skills. Encouraging them to identify problems, brainstorm solutions, and evaluate the outcomes will empower them to overcome obstacles independently.

Building strong support networks is also essential for developing resilience in children. Encourage healthy relationships with family members, friends, teachers, or mentors who can provide guidance and emotional support during difficult times.

Additionally, helping children cultivate self-compassion is vital for developing resilience. Teaching them how to practice self-care and acknowledge their own strengths and weaknesses will enable them to approach challenges with self-assurance.

Promoting positive coping strategies such as mindfulness exercises or engaging in hobbies they enjoy can significantly contribute to building resilience in children.

By teaching these valuable skills at an early age, we are equipping our future generation with the tools they need not only survive but thrive in an ever-changing world.

CONCLUSION

In the depths of our struggles, when self-sabotage, depression, and anxiety seem to consume every ounce of our being, it is easy to lose sight of the light at the end of the tunnel. But dear readers, never forget that even in these darkest moments, there is always room for encouragement and hope. Allow this glimmering flame to guide you towards a path where inspiration awaits.

Believe in your own strength and resilience; know that you possess the power to overcome any obstacle that dares cross your path. Embrace each challenge as an opportunity for growth rather than succumbing to its weight. Harness your inner courage and take those first brave steps towards reclaiming your life from the unforgiving clutches of self-doubt.

Hold steadfastly onto hope like a lifeline; let its warmth envelop you during those moments when darkness threatens to suffocate your spirit. The road ahead may be winding and treacherous, fraught with setbacks and doubts; yet within each setback lies an opportunity for comebacks greater than ever imagined before. So muster all your strength, summon all the faith left within you—because there is nothing more powerful than one's determination combined with hope!

BOOKS BY THIS AUTHOR

Anxiety: Find Relief Naturally

"Find Peace from Anxiety Naturally and Transform Your Life"
We all suffer from anxiety from time to time in our lives, but for some of us, it can be a daily struggle. Anxiety can lead to a multitude of health issues including, sleep disturbances, increased blood pressure, irritability, extreme fatigue, relationship issues, and more - all leading to even more anxiety!

Bath And Body Business: A Girl's Guide To Starting A Homebased Business

Bath and Body Business: A Girl's Guide to Starting a Homebased Business

This book was written by an experienced business owner who shares her creative path to starting a successful business from home. You will learn the basics to get you up and running quickly and efficiently.

Manifesting Prosperity: A Guide To Creating Real Prosperity With Intentional Thought

Everything you encounter is your creation. In other words, you create your reality! There is a spiritual and energy force connecting everything in the universe. You construct your reality through this connected energy of all visible and invisible objects.

This potent creative energy from within you shapes and forms the universe around you. This book will guide you on how to recognize your thoughts, apply the "law of attraction" to create your reality, enhance your energy frequency, and change your negative ideas and perspective to materialize abundance and prosperity!

Priestess: Mysteries Of The Divine Feminine

Priestesses hold an important place in many ancient cultures, serving as spiritual leaders, healers, and guardians of ancient traditions. These women played a vital role in connecting communities with their religious beliefs, acting as intermediaries between the mortal and divine realms.

Crystals For Beginners: Discover The Healing And Magical Energies Of Crystals And Stones

Discover the Healing and Magical Energies of Crystals, Stones, and Crystal Grids.

Topics Include:
~Understanding Crystals
~Selecting and Caring for your crystals
~Harnessing the power of crystals
~Crystal Grids
~Popular Crystals and Stones
~Using Crystals in Meditation
~Popular Crystal Pairings